MW01025581

Fly Fishing
in North Carolina

Buck Paysour

DOWN HOME

Down Home Press
Asheboro, N.C.

Copyright © 1995 by Buck Paysour

First printing, April, 1995

All rights reserved. No part of this book may be reproduced by any means without permission from the publisher, except for brief passages in reviews and articles.

ISBN 1-878086-38-3

Library of Congress Number 95-067569

Printed in the United States of America

Cover photograph courtesy
North Carolina Travel and Tourism Division

Book design by Katrina Breitenbach

2 3 4 5 6 7 8 9 10

Down Home Press
PO Box 4126
Asheboro, N.C. 27204

To

Alice Love

and

Helen Sanford Wilhelm,

high school English teachers who instilled in me a love for books, words, and writing—even though they understood that I would rather be fishing than incarcerated in class. Any bad writing in this book is not their fault. They taught me better. No doubt they also expected me to write a great novel some day. Maybe even at my age there is still time....

Foreword

I love everything about fishing. I love just thinking about going, and I love getting ready to go, making the plans, organizing the gear. The night before a fishing trip can be as exciting to us grown-up little boys as Christmas Eve.

Memories of earlier fishing trips often crop up then, making the anticipation and excitement even greater. Memories of that huge bass that clobbered a topwater bug on a farm pond early one morning, giving you a fight like no other. Or that rainbow trout that snatched a fly on a fast, cold-running stream while you struggled not to slip on the slimy rocks and fall in over your waders so you wouldn't provoke laughter from your buddies and create a fishing tale that you'd hear forever.

I even like coming home from fishing. That may sound strange to some, but when my friends and I go fishing, we usually are fortunate enough to catch enough to eat. And second only to catching fish, I like to eat them. I love fried bream and trout and all the other fish we catch. I even eat the fins and tails, leaving only the head—and not all of it.

I've fished in many beautiful spots around the world, but no place overshadows our own North Carolina waters, especially High Rock Lake and the Davidson County farm ponds where I did my first fishing. No one ever told me when I caught my first fish, but I'm sure it had to have been with my Dad, my older brother, Tim, and Baxter Everhart, who worked with my Dad and whom I called Mr. Bax. Mr. Bax loved fishing more than anybody I ever knew, and I can remember sitting on his knee, holding a cane pole, waiting for the bobber to go under.

I don't remember when I learned to fly fish either, but I'm sure that those three must have been there, because I've been fly fishing since I could hold a rod.

I can't stir my fishing memories without also mentioning two other fishing companions from my youth: "Punkin" Wallace, who loved to fish as much as I did, and whose ashes now rest in the Yadkin River he loved; and the Reverend Howard Wilkinson, our Methodist minister in Lexington when I was a teenager—boy, did he love to fish. I had some great times fishing with them, and with many good fishing friends since.

All of my vivid memories of fishing, from childhood to the present, are re-kindled in this wonderful book. Buck Paysour is as skillful with words on the end of a pen as the best fisherman is with a fly on the end of a line. In the best sense of the phrase, he "takes us with him," and we feel the strike of that robin redbreast on the Lumber River, or the excitement of hooking that brown trout on the South Toe.

This book is filled not only with practical advice for fly fishing North Carolina waters, but also with the instinctual appreciation for the "personalities" of each stream and of each fish found there. It is advice that comes from a lifetime of loving to fish these native waters...advice born out of loving, careful observation and experience, rather than mere research. As an artist, as well as a fly fisherman, I can appreciate that.

This book is a "must read" for every fly fisherman, but anyone who appreciates this state's grand and subtle natural beauty will delight in "climbing in" and going fly fishing with Buck Paysour.

Bob Timberlake

Acknowledgements

So many people have contributed directly or indirectly to this book that it is impossible for me to remember them all. For that reason, I hesitate to attempt to name them because that is what it will be: just an attempt. In fact, some people who have helped don't even realize it. For that reason, I will miss some. Even so, I am so grateful to everyone who helped either directly or indirectly that I feel I should make an attempt to name as many as possible. So here goes.

I am especially grateful to Jerry Bledsoe, my publisher, my editor, my friend, and good fishing buddy, for having enough faith in me to bring this book and one of my previous books to life. I am also particularly grateful to all the anglers whose names appear elsewhere in the book; without them, there would be no book. And, of course, I never could have written this book without the understanding and advice of Doris Dale. In my last two fishing books, I described her as "my best catch." She still is and will always be. My older son, John, and his wife, Kim, and my younger son, Conrad, and his wife, Jan, have given me many happy hours of companionship, fishing and otherwise, and are due much credit for this book as well.

Others who contributed include Leger Meyland, a fine photographer and a very good friend who helped me with many of the photographs that appear in the book; Eddie Bridges, a good friend, a fine all-around sportsman and former N.C. Wildlife Resources Commission Commissioner; Avery Freeman and Tom Sawyer, two great fishermen; Hugh Page, former colleague on the Greensboro *News & Record*; Charlie Whichard, a friend whose counsel has helped me stretch my limited income to the point where I could afford to retire from my full-time work early and write exclusively about fishing—and even to fish myself from time to time; and to publisher Bill Kennedy and the other folks at *ESP* magazine in Greensboro; Robert Warren of the *High Point Enterprise*.

Still others who have directly or indirectly contributed include: two very dear friends, Greta and Woody Tilley, who have helped make even fishless and near-fishless fishing trips fun and who have made just living more wonderful for Doris Dale and me; Rusty and Ross Angel; Gerry Broome and John Page, Greensboro *News & Record* photographers; Hubert Breeze, a good fishing buddy who remained a friend even through the time he was my editor; John Robinson, who always treated me decently even though he was an editor who never fished with me; and Buzz Bryson of Raleigh; Gene Vann of Greensboro, who not only delivers our mail but also delivers news about fishing; W.C. Idol; and a good friend, Curtis Laughlin.

Also, Ervin Jackson of Charlotte, Ben Douglas of Wilson; members of the Nat Greene Fly Fishers; Jack Spruill of Winston-Salem; Warren Dixon of Liberty; Abe Jones, former colleague on the Greensboro *News & Record*; Tom Higgins of the *Charlotte Observer*; David Hastings of Lexington; Lebby Lamb, head of the reference department of the Greensboro Public Library and her reference librarians: Frank Barefoot, Stephen Culkin, Becky Floyd, Bob Foster, Bobby Hollandsworth, Doug Kerr, Belinda Lam, Bessie Nkonge, and John Owens, all of whom have helped me when I have been trying to find out such things as whether white bass are in the same family as white perch, which they are.

Contents

Preface

I began work on this book with much apprehension and almost abandoned it in frustration. Now, as I near the end of the project, I realize it has been by far the most difficult thing I have ever written. Part of the reason is that throughout the writing I was cognizant of the fact that the average fly fisherman is highly literate and intelligent. If I made mistakes, I knew, I would hear about it. But my trepidation at writing about fly fishing was tempered by one fact: fly rod anglers are not snobs and will forgive you—once they have pointed out your errors.

Another reason for my doubts about writing a book on North Carolina fly fishing was that I knew I might feel like a charlatan, because I am not among the best fly rod anglers in North Carolina. I am not even among the best in my home county of Guilford, or in my home town of Greensboro. I'm not even among the best in my circle of fly fishing friends.

But then I thought about an exchange I sometimes have when I fish with Wilt Browning, a friend who writes sports for the Greensboro *News & Record*. When I haven't caught anything for a long time, he kids me.

"You should be catching something," he says. "After all, you wrote the book on North Carolina fishing."

I always have the same answer.

"Well, you write about football and you haven't ever won a Heisman Trophy have you?"

But somehow that doesn't keep Wilt from giving me a hard time about my fishing. I hope it never does.

I do have enough skill with the fly rod to catch fish, sometimes many of them. I have caught my share of largemouth bass on a fly rod in the several decades since I learned to use it. I have caught fewer North Carolina mountain trout during that time, but I was using a fly rod when I caught all that I did catch. Only in Virginia have I caught mountain trout on anything but a fly rod, and that shouldn't count as far as this book goes.

And even though I am not the best fly fisherman in the world, few other people have as much enthusiasm for the fly rod. I may, in fact, be the only person in the United States who caught three nice largemouth bass on a fly rod the morning after suffering a heart attack.

That is no fish tale. I have witnesses.

With apologies to those who have read my *Bass Fishing in North Carolina*, here is how that happened:

We were fishing Currituck Sound in mid-June. It was one of those uncommon days on the sound when there was no breeze. The sun beat down unmercifully and was hurled back in our faces by the mirror-calm water. I thought I was going to pass out from a heat stroke. The first day, I caught five or six nice bass and was happy even though my eyes stung with sweat, and I could hardly breathe. After we returned to the motel where we were staying, my chest felt tight, and my stomach began to ache and churn. Thinking that I had severe indigestion, I drank a half pint of milk and munched Rolaids. Still, the pain and constriction in my chest worsened. I lost my lunch.

Roger Soles, my fishing partner for the day, wanted to take me to a doctor. Continuing to believe that my problem was just an upset stomach, I refused to go. Whereupon Roger went back into his room, which adjoined mine, to take a shower. I walked outside to get some fresh air.

A new wave of nausea engulfed me and, for the first time, I suspected it could be a heart attack. I had long known I was a candidate for one; my mother and father both died young from heart problems. So I finally agreed to let Cecil Martin, who had already finished his shower and was outside waiting to go to dinner, drive me to a clinic in the village of Jarvisburg. It was then well after normal office hours, and Dr. Charles Wright, the clinic's owner, was not in. Cecil suggested we drive to the hospital in Elizabeth City. By this time, however, the nausea and discomfort had again subsided. Once more I rationalized that the problem was just heartburn.

We returned to our lodgings, and I ate a bowl of oyster stew for dinner; I did not feel like eating a full meal. The next morning, I experienced extreme ennui. Yet I went out on the sound and caught three bass on a yellow popping bug and a nine-foot graphite rod, both of which I had lovingly made the past winter.

We quit fishing at noon, as we had planned to do all along, and started the drive back to our Greensboro homes. I continued to feel miserable. When we stopped in Warrenton for dinner, I only picked at my barbecue.

Back in my own bed that night, I slept fitfully. I had taken several more days of vacation so I could go fishing with my older son, John, who was scheduled to be home on leave from the Air Force. The next day, I still felt queasy and drove to Dr. William Gray Murray's office.

"You've had a heart attack, and you're having one right now," he said after studying the electrocardiogram.

He dispatched me to Wesley Long Hospital's emergency room, where nurses monitored me for a couple of hours before admitting me to the intensive care unit.

That night, Dr. Murray came by my room, patted my left foot, and said, "You're a very lucky man."

Until then, I had thought the three bass I caught the day before had been the result of my skill with a fly rod. Not luck.

Yet another reason I was reluctant to write a book on North Carolina fly fishing is that much mystique surrounds fly fishing. Many anglers hesitate to try it because they think it too difficult. They believe it requires great facility and coordination. Not so. It took my son, John, only a short time to learn to use a fly rod well enough to catch bass, and he was barely twelve at the time. Sure, he has much more coordination than I; he rode a bicycle the first time he tried and learned to water-ski in less than an hour.

I, on the other hand, am so lubberly that when I dance, I not only stumble over my partner's feet, I get tripped up in my own. Yet I have caught many fish on a fly rod since I first picked one up late in life. Admittedly, it took much time and effort for me to learn. My wife, Doris Dale, no doubt wishes I would devote as much energy to learning to dance.

A friend who is an avid golfer, Ed Satterfield, has a sign on his office wall that refers to golf but could be about fly fishing. It reads:

Golf is like sex. You don't have to be good at it to enjoy it.

True, there is a certain elegance to fly fishing. Done with perfection, it is, as some have described it, "poetry in motion."

Come to think about it, the same thing could be said about sex.

If it had not been for a fishing buddy and good personal friend, Bill Black, I may not have had enough audacity to finish writing this book. He did more than encourage me; he insisted that I finish it. He began his campaign when he, John Baskervill, and I stopped in North Wilkesboro to eat dinner on the way home from a New River fly-fishing expedition for smallmouth bass. During the meal, the subject turned to—what else?—fly fishing. Bill said he thought there was a need for a book on North Carolina fly fishing. Then he added that I should finish the one I had started to write several years before but had given up after finding it so forbidding. Later, Bill telephoned several times to urge that I get back to work on the book. Just about every time that Doris Dale and I had dinner with Bill and Jo Ann after that, or when Bill and I fished together, or when we just talked, he asked what progress I had made on the book and exhorted me to keep plugging away.

Bill, who was then a banker but has since retired and now fishes as often as he can, is very persuasive—as are most bankers. The more I thought about it, the more I realized he was right about the need for a book on North Carolina fly fishing. Because of its location and climate, our state has a greater variety of fish than any other state in the union. And most of these—from sea trout to mountain trout, from puppy drum to pumpkinseed bream and from striped bass to smallmouth and largemouth bass—can be caught on a fly rod.

Yet, as best as I can determine, no one had ever written a book on all the varied types of North Carolina fly fishing.

5

So, at Bill's urging, I once more cranked up my computer and set about finishing what I had started several years before. I soon realized, however, that there was no way to write about every species that can be caught on fly rods in North Carolina. To do that, a book would be as unwieldy as a Number Twelve sinking line on a five-foot, one-ounce fly rod. For that reason, I chose to write about only the most representative of sports fishes that can be caught on a fly rod.

That's why you won't find much about such fish as gar, carp and catfish in the pages that follow. Don't laugh. All have been caught in our state on fly rods. While fishing the Pungo River, my friend John Peterson caught a large carp on a small wet fly. John probably wishes he had never caught that fish; over the years, he has had to endure much ribbing about it.

I quit kidding him after something that happened to me while I was fishing a Guilford County lake with Bill Bennett and Burt Massengale. We were fishing for bream, and I was using a Woolly Worm that I had tied myself and a seven-foot, reed-thin fly rod.

Bill and I fished from a boat while Burt, as he usually does, fished with crickets from the bank.

Bill quietly rowed me back into a cove and said, "This is a good spot."

I flipped my Woolly Worm to the left side of a pine tree that had fallen into the water.

Just as I was about to make a back cast to shoot my bug to the other side of the tree, my floating fly line zipped across the water. I leaned back to set the hook and felt the lunge of a strong fish against the rod, a rod that weighed only about two ounces. The fight was on.

After I battled the fish for two minutes or so, Bill Bennett said, "I don't believe that's a bass. A bass would have already come to the top."

I knew he was right, and I began to believe that I had hooked the world-record bream. Dreams of how I could exploit my triumph raced through my head.

Cortland Line Company, which made both the seven-foot rod and the Size Four line that I was using, would pay me to endorse its products. Berkley Incorporated, manufacturer of my reel, would give me a fat contract in return for permission to use a photograph of me holding up my monster bream. Briefly I thought about marketing, under the name "Buck's Worm," the fly I had tied. But somehow that didn't seem appropriate. I decided instead to give it the name that Curtis Youngblood has given to the fly-rod poppers that I make: "Big Bad Buck's Bug." No matter what I named it, I reasoned, anglers would buy duplicates of it in hopes that they, too, could catch such a huge bream. I continued battling my "world record bream," which played tug of war with me, first ripping off line, then letting me gain a little line before taking off again. Later, when I thought I had won the contest, the fish began racing from one side of the boat to the other.

My leader only tested at four pounds, and I was afraid to be too aggressive lest it shatter.

After what seemed like hours—it was probably closer to five minutes—I worked the fish to the top of the water and Bill scooped it up. He carefully removed my fly and released a big catfish, which flipped its tail and swam away with my dreams of fame and riches.

I mentioned the gar a page or so back because I once even caught one, a large one, on a fly rod. My younger son, Conrad, and I were fishing for largemouth bass in Scranton

Creek near Conrad's Belhaven home when we saw legions of fish slashing the surface.

"Bass!" I yelled.

It was understandable why I assumed the fish were bass. In the past, I had caught many largemouth that were schooling on the top of that stretch of the creek.

Conrad and I excitedly cast into the swirls. I let my red, black and yellow bass bug rest on the surface for a second, twitched it a couple of times, then let it sit again for a moment. Its feather and rubber legs wiggled, making it look like some gaudy frog or insect. Suddenly, the bug disappeared, leaving a cavity where it had been. I thought I had a gigantic bass until I worked it close enough to the boat to see its long and wicked bill, which identified it as an alligator gar. Catching it was fun.

Tom Kirkman has caught many kinds of both game fish and non-game fish on a fly rod in North Carolina and has enjoyed catching every one. He even admires the carp.

"A carp puts up a good scrap," the High Point angler and builder of fine fishing rods says. "But I have been with people who have hooked carp and talked about what good fighting fish they were—until they got the fish close enough to the boat to see what they were. Then they are disappointed."

Tom can not understand this attitude. If an angler thinks a fish is a pleasure to catch, why should the angler turn up his or her nose at the fish upon discovering it is not one of the more classic species?

Tom has even caught mudfish (also known as bowfin or grinnel) on a fly rod and had fun doing it.

"They leap like tarpon," he says.

Tom is apparently not the only person who admires the fighting spirit of mudfish. In some places, they are called by the more sophisticated name "cypress trout."

So don't malign any fish you catch on a fly rod.

But don't expect to see much more about gar, carp, catfish, or mudfish in this book.

Yes, it's impossible to cover, in one book, every species of fish that you can take on a fly rod in our state. In fact, I can't even cover all the North Carolina game fish that will hit a fly, streamer, or popper.

That's why, in thinking further about what this book should accomplish, I also decided to restrict its scope primarily to fresh and brackish water fly fishing, venturing only peripherally into saltwater fly fishing. Accordingly, you will find nothing about fishing for large saltwater species such as marlin—fish you have to trick to come within striking distance of your lure and then, to land the fish, use fly rods so stiff and heavy they have been facetiously compared to telephone poles.

I have instead elected to write mostly about North Carolina fish that can be taken in fresh and brackish water on fly tackle of reasonable size by anglers who have reasonable skill and who wade or fish from the bank or from a boat of modest size. This rules out tarpon, a fish that can and have been caught on fly rods in North Carolina on rare occasions.

I have, however, elected to write about some species of fish, such as speckled sea trout, that are not commonly caught on fly rods—probably because not many people fish for them with fly rods. But some people do fish for them and catch them with fly rods. Even I have caught some small ones on flies. Besides, sea trout are so intriguing that fly fishing for them makes an interesting story.

Among the other things that you won't find in this book are surf fishing or other ocean fishing with a fly rod. That subject is for another book. When I do discuss pure salt water, which is only occasionally, it will be water that is relatively sheltered, such as the stretch of the White Oak River north of Swansboro (see Chapters Two, Three, Fourteen, and Fifteen). In other words, I only discuss saltwater fly fishing that can be done with the same rod and the same boat that you might use to fish for largemouth bass.

Nor does this book encompass fly fishing for such North Carolina freshwater fish as the muskellunge and others that are seldom taken by fly rod.

This still leaves a great variety of fish to be caught on a fly rod in fresh water, brackish water and sheltered salt water. Brackish water, incidentally, often holds both saltwater and freshwater species (see Chapter Fourteen), many of which will hit a streamer fly or a fly rod popper.

Something else you won't find in this book is anything about techniques or mechanics, such as how to cast a fly rod. To learn that, you should seek out a mentor such as my friend Bill Wilkerson, a fine teacher of fly rod techniques, or join a fly fishing club, or attend one of the fly fishing schools that many fly fishing equipment mail order companies offer. Or you can read some other book as well as this one. In the Greensboro Public Library alone, there are more than forty books on fly fishing. My personal library contains several dozen such books. Many of those tell you how to make a conventional cast, a false cast, or a roll cast, or how to do the single haul, double haul, or about any other cast you care to try. Some will also give you advice on fly tying, how to make your own leaders, and how to tie knots you may need for fly fishing. (See Appendix A for a selection of books that could be helpful to both beginning and veteran fly rod anglers.) But I could uncover no book that tells you how, when, and where to catch the great variety of fish that can be taken on a fly rod in the brackish and fresh waters of North Carolina. In this book, with much help from some fine North Carolina fly rod anglers, I hope to tell you something about fly rod fishing in our state.

Speaking of help from other fly rod anglers, this volume is essentially a task of reporting information that I have gathered from others. However, the bulk of the work is also basically a first-person account. I have written it that way despite the fact that I am now, and probably always will be, an average fly fisherman. I have included many personal observations and recollections partly because that was the most natural way to write it. Besides, I have had so many interesting and pleasurable days of fishing with my fly rod that I enjoyed reliving them.

Photo by Buck Paysour

Bill Black uses a homemade wading staff to probe his way along the New River while fishing for smallmouth bass.

Chapter One

There's No Place Like Home

It is an early morning in October. The woods around Lake Brandt, just a few miles from my Greensboro home, are alive with the chirping of birds, the rustling of squirrels, and the buzzing of insects. A mallard drake flies so low over my fourteen-foot aluminum skiff that I can see its iridescent blue epaulets and hear the soft whir of its wings.

The sun has been up only a short while and it casts a blush on the water and in the mist rising from the water. I flip my fly rod popping bug next to a partially submerged willow and let it lie motionless a moment until the rings it has made disappear. Then I jiggle the bug. There is a detonation that makes a noise like a firecracker exploding under water. The bug disappears, and I lean back to set the hook. A largemouth bass hurdles from the water.

I land and release the bass and silently thank all the fishermen I have ever known for adding so much to my life. But I thank, most of all, every fly fisherman I have known—especially Roger Soles and Bodie McDowell. They convinced me that even I—who can barely rub my head and pat my stomach at the same time—could learn to use a fly rod.

There are certain fish that forever stand out in a fisherman's memories. Mine include my first fish—a robin redbreast I caught on a nightcrawler and a cane pole on the Catawba River when I was just a few years old; my first largemouth bass, a nine-pound, fourteen-ounce one I caught while trolling with my dad and the late Roscoe "Sweeney" Kennington on Lake Murray, South Carolina, when I was about eight years old; my first striped bass, a relatively small one that hit a broken-back Rebel lure on Pantego Creek in Eastern North Carolina; and the first largemouth bass I ever caught on a fly rod.

Of all these, my first fish—the tiny redbreast—gave me the biggest kick. But there is no doubt about which one afforded me my second greatest fishing thrill. It was the first largemouth bass that I caught on a fly rod. Although I had been fishing most of my life, I learned to use the fly rod only when I was approaching age forty. And although I had tried for several months to catch bass on my new cheap yellow fiberglass fly rod, I had managed to catch only a few small bream, and had difficulty keeping my line tight enough to hook them. Then I made my first trip to Currituck Sound.

The vast and shallow sound was, at that time, one of the best places in the world to catch bass—especially on a fly rod and a popping bug. But on this trip, Currituck was not to live up to its reputation. Not even Roger Soles, the best largemouth bass fly rod fisherman I've ever known, could catch a fish.

The culprit: the wind that had blown hard from the northeast for several days before we arrived. Currituck, despite its closeness to the ocean, has no lunar tide. But it does have what many older Currituck County natives describe, in their Elizabethan brogue, as a "wind tuyoide." A nor'easter drives much of the water out of the sound and into Albemarle Sound to the south. Currituck, shallow even under the best of circumstances, is exceedingly difficult to fish when that happens.

I flailed the air with my fly rod until I felt as if my arm was going to break but did not get even a sniff from a bass.

At lunch on the second day, our last day of fishing, Roger suggested I switch to a casting rod and try a Johnson Silver spoon dressed with a rubber skirt or a pork rind strip. I took his advice and caught a nice bass, the only one anybody in our party had caught up until then. I was proud of the fish but disappointed that I did not catch it on a fly rod. I had caught many bass in my life but until then, never one on a fly rod.

That evening, the wind shifted and began to stream from the southwest. Water rushed back into the sound. It happened almost too late for us; we were planning to return to Greensboro early the next morning. After dinner, just to have something to do, Jack Bilyeu proposed that he and I fish a creek that runs off the sound near the fishing lodge where we were staying. I agreed.

Jack asked Grover Cleveland "G.C." Sawyer, Jr., a fishing guide and owner of the fishing lodge, if we could borrow one of his boats. Sure, he answered, and Jack and I sauntered down to the creek and loaded our fly rods in one of G.C.'s skiffs. Jack poled the skiff to the middle of the creek, and we flipped our bass bugs to the edge of a grass bed.

I was pessimistic. But after about my fifteenth cast, I let my yellow and black bug sit for a minute, then popped it a couple of times, and let it sit again. When I turned to Jack to say something, I heard a commotion in the direction of my bug and whirled around to look. My bug had departed, and there was nothing but a miniature whirlpool where it had once been. I leaned back to set the hook and a big bass bounded into the air. My heart raced, but I managed to work the fish to the boat where Jack slipped the landing net under it. It was a beautiful bass, made even more beautiful because it was the first I had ever caught on a fly rod.

The bass was the only one anybody in our party of six caught on a fly rod in two days of fishing. It was to be one of only two times in many fishing trips that I would catch more fish than Roger Soles.

Looking back, I don't think I caught that bass. Instead, that bass caught me, because I have been hooked on fly fishing ever since.

The reason I owe Roger Soles an enormous debt is that he taught me to use a fly rod. He was then a vice president of Jefferson Standard Life Insurance Co., a predecessor to Jefferson-Pilot Corporation, a company he was to later run. He came in one day to Wilkerson's Drug Store in downtown Greensboro where I took morning coffee breaks, sat down beside me at the counter, and ordered a cup of coffee. I did not know him then, but we exchanged pleasantries. When he learned I liked to fish, he said fishing was also one of his favorite pastimes. I asked what kind of fishing he liked best.

"Bass fishing with a fly rod," he answered.

I told him that I had bought my first fly rod a few weeks earlier and was having difficulty learning to use it. Soon after that, Roger invited Doris Dale and me to his and Majelle's house. He brought out his fly rod. Then, while our wives socialized, he and I went out into his backyard where he showed me how to fly cast.

A few days later, Bodie McDowell accompanied me to the parking lot of the old *Greensboro Daily News* building and taught me to do the "double haul," a technique that allows you to shoot your fly line without wasted motion. When the double haul is done properly, you can feel the line zip through your outstretched palm as it flows out to your target. Bodie was then outdoors editor of the *Greensboro Daily News*. He later joined the North Carolina Wildlife Commission.

Roger and Bodie added much to my life with their lessons. Over the years, fly fishing has given me enormous pleasure. The only thing I regret about learning to use the fly rod is that I didn't do it when I was young instead of waiting until I was nearing middle age.

Living in North Carolina is one thing I will never regret. There is no other state that offers more diverse fly fishing.

As Tom Kirkman of High Point, a very good fly fisherman, says, "The fishing we have here puts Florida's to shame. In fact, there is nowhere else in the world where you can catch the variety of fish that we have here."

It's interesting that Tom should say that North Carolina fishing "puts Florida's to shame," because an increasing number of Floridians are moving to North Carolina, especially to the mountains. Mountain trout is what brings some of them to Western North Carolina.

Trout fishing did not bring Roger Caylor, a Floridian, to the North Carolina mountains, but it—and a pretty, young mountain woman—kept him there.

Roger came to Watauga County from Pensacola in the early 1980s for what was supposed to be a temporary job doing such things as stringing cable for an oil exploration project.

But after he arrived, he met and courted and, after a while, married Malidean Main of Watauga County. He also discovered fly fishing for mountain trout, something that at first did not go as smoothly as his romance with Malidean. As do most beginning fly fishermen, he lost many of his artificial flies. He snapped them off on his back casts. He broke them off on overhanging bushes. They hung on rocks. Occasionally, he even lost one to a big trout.

"I decided I could not afford to keep on fly fishing unless I learned to make my own flies," he recalls.

17

So he took some fly tying courses at the High Country Fly Fishing shop near his home.

Saving money was not the only incentive Roger had to take up fly tying as a hobby.

"I needed something to do in the winter," he recalls. "The snow really piles up up here."

He and his family live in a beautiful but rugged and sparsely populated area of northern Watauga County on Meat Camp Creek. Their community, like the creek, is known as Meat Camp because it was a place where early hunters and trappers, including Daniel Boone, brought hides and salted meat to sell.

After a couple of winters, Roger became so skilled at fly tying that High Country Fly Fishing Shop owner Al Hines suggested that Roger try producing some flies to sell.

Roger took Al's advice and sold a few flies. Fishermen who bought them caught trout on them. Word about the flies spread. Today, he makes his living tying and selling flies. Malidean helps him.

Most of the flies Roger ties are for trout fishing and he still finds time to use some of them himself. He does tie some for other kinds of fishing, especially for smallmouth and largemouth bass. He takes some of the streamers he makes—such things as Zonkers and Woolly Buggers—with him when he visits his hometown of Pensacola, Florida. There, he catches largemouth bass and chain pickerel and a few other species on them.

Even though he enjoys his visits to Florida, he has no intentions of permanently moving back there. He is too fond of the North Carolina mountains.

"I never get tired of sitting here and looking at that mountain," he says as he points from his front porch toward Snake Mountain.

Nor does he think he will ever get tired of North Carolina fly fishing.

Mountain trout fishing is just one of many kinds of fly fishing that North Carolina offers. In the mountains, we have not only the trout streams that Roger Caylor and other fly fishermen love, but also whitewater smallmouth bass rivers that you can fish from a canoe or by wading. We have deep mountain lakes where you can also fish for bass and other species by using sinking fly lines to fish deep, or floating lines and dry flies and bass poppers to fish the surface, or sinking flies to fish several feet under the surface. There is also, much to the surprise of many flatland anglers, some very good bream fishing on the mountain lakes.

In the booming Piedmont, anglers catch big bream and other panfish, white bass, striped bass, largemouth bass, and several other species of fish on fly rods.

In Eastern North Carolina, you catch most species that you can catch in the Piedmont—and more. In the brackish-water creeks, rivers and sounds, you can sometimes catch both saltwater fish and freshwater fish (see Chapter Fourteen) in the same water.

Dave Goforth, one of the state's best all-around fishermen, often talked about this.

"I've even seen porpoises in water where I was fishing for freshwater fish," he said. "If you want to catch both freshwater and saltwater fish, the tributaries off the Pamlico Sound are the best places to do it, and fall is the best time to do it."

I had my first experience catching saltwater and freshwater fish in the same water one fall day about twenty years ago when Jack Rochelle of High Point and Florida and I fished Pungo Creek in Eastern North Carolina. On that trip, we caught bass after bass on fly rods. When my arm became

19

tired from whipping the fly rod, I switched to an ultralight spinning rod and caught both flounder and white perch on a Mepps spinner, right in the same water where we had caught those largemouth on fly rods. I later learned that we could have caught the perch and flounder on fly rods and a spinner fly, similar to what we were using on the spinning rods but lighter, or on other sinking fly rod lures.

On another fall day while fishing with Curtis Youngblood, I eased my boat up to the mouth of Mill Creek to within casting distance of where I knew there were submerged logs. Then I picked up my fly rod and cast a popper to the top of the logs. As soon as the bug hit the water, something grabbed it. A small largemouth bass—a freshwater fish, of course—bolted from the water and threw the bug.

I had not moved the boat a foot when Curtis's spinning rod bent.

"You must have a nice bass there," I yelled, scrambling for the landing net.

After Curtis had worked the fish close to the boat, we could see a spot on its tail, a spot that identified it as a nice puppy drum, a saltwater fish. Curtis landed the puppy drum and later made a fine meal of it. I was still ignorant of the fact that the puppy drum would have hit the right kind of fly rod lure.

Mill Creek is a stream that runs into Pungo Creek, which in turn is a tributary to the Pungo River, which flows into the Pamlico River, which flows into the Pamlico Sound, which finally flows into the Atlantic Ocean. Although Mill Creek is many miles from the ocean, enough salt water seeps from Pamlico Sound into the creek to make it habitable to several species of saltwater fish. Yet, during periods of normal rainfall, it remains fresh enough to accommodate many species of freshwater fish.

On still another fall day, I watched as Bill Black caught an astonishing variety of both freshwater and saltwater fish on Back Creek at Bath. He caught bluegill bream, croaker, flounder, largemouth bass, puppy drum, white perch, yellow perch, and others. He caught most of those fish, including all the saltwater species, on a spinning rod. But we also caught several species of freshwater fish, including bass, on fly rods—all in the same water.

Since that day, I have experienced the joys of "mixed bag fishing" (see Chapter Fourteen) many times in Eastern North Carolina.

In addition to fresh and saltwater fish, Eastern North Carolina's fresh and brackish waters also from time to time hold anadromous species—fish that live part of their lives in salt water and part in fresh water. "Anadromous" comes from a Greek word that loosely means "running up into." Hence anadromous fish swim up into fresh or brackish water rivers and sounds from the ocean, usually to spawn. Species that do this include shad and striped bass.

Many saltwater and anadromous species that inhabit North Carolina brackish water can be caught on a fly rod and on many of the same flies, streamers or poppers that you use for freshwater fish. This adds to the suspense of a trip. You never know what will nail your popping bug, streamer or other fly rod lure on your next cast....

Even though you won't find anything much about fly casting or similar techniques in this book, you should, if you have never fly fished before, know something about the equipment you need to fish North Carolina.

First, a word about rods. There is no such thing as the perfect fly rod for fishing all of North Carolina. Still, an eight-foot rod matched for a seven-weight line is a good choice for North Carolina fishing if you plan to acquire only one rod until you decide that you like fly fishing enough to invest more money.

"One reason that would be a good rod to start out with is that it is easier for a beginner to get his timing down with a little heavier line," says Don Howell of Brevard, a fine fly fisherman. "You need to feel the line when it straightens out on your back cast, and you can feel a heavier line better."

(The higher the number that a fly line is, the heavier it is. A Number Two line, for example, is very light and a Number Eleven, very heavy.)

There is another reason an eight-foot rod matched for a Number Seven line is a good outfit to start out with. It will handle about any reasonable-size fish that can be caught in the sheltered fresh and brackish waters of North Carolina— from mountain trout to sea trout, from bream to smallmouth and largemouth bass, and from small striped bass to small puppy drum.

By shopping carefully, you should be able to purchase your first fly fishing outfit for under $300 if you stick with a modest-priced rod. The outfit should include a graphite rod, a reel, a line, leaders, and a few flies, streamers and popping bugs.

In the beginning, you can scrimp on the reel. For most bass, trout, and panfish fishing, the reel is the least important part of a fly fishing outfit. It is merely a device on which to store line. You land most medium-size freshwater fish by stripping the line in with your hand. I once fished with Roger Soles when the foot on his reel broke so that the reel would not stay on his rod. Roger simply placed the reel in the bottom of the boat and continued to catch largemouth bass.

Although you need a sturdy reel if you want to go after larger fish, about any "single-action" reel balanced for your rod will work for your first fly reel. A single-action reel is one that retrieves line at the rate of one turn of line for each turn of the handle and does not automatically retrieve line.

Use the money you save on the reel to help you buy the best fly line you can afford. The fly line is important. It carries out your fly or other fly rod lure. In other types of fishing, such as spinning and baitcasting, the lure carries your line out. If you buy that eight-foot, seven-weight rod as your first one, your best bet is a floating bass bug or saltwater taper line. Many good fly fishermen I know rarely use sinking lines although my friend Bill Wilkerson thinks experienced anglers who do not use sinking lines under certain conditions are making a mistake.

"I believe that with the explosion of fly fishing, North Carolina anglers will eventually begin using more sinking lines," he says.

Certainly, however, beginning fly rod anglers should stick with a floating line for their first line for North Carolina fishing.

A bass or saltwater taper is one that has a short small front end and a thick belly just behind the front, then a longer section of smaller running line. Because most of the weight is concentrated toward the front, it is easier to cast— especially in the wind. Yet its smaller front end allows it to land on the water without too much of a splash.

But a tapered line is relatively expensive. So if you are not sure you are going to enjoy fly fishing enough to stick with it, you can get along with a level floating line. A level line is one that has the same thickness and weight throughout. It costs less yet casts reasonably well under normal conditions. But it creates a little more disturbance when it hits the water than does a tapered line.

A double-tapered line will probably be the second line you buy. Although it sometimes costs a little more than a level line, it usually is not as expensive as a weight-forward line. A double-tapered line has exactly the same front and rear. Its belly, or middle, is relatively heavy and its front and rear lighter and smaller. Because it has a small front, it does not make the commotion on the water that a level line makes. Yet the thick middle section of the double taper line makes it easier to cast than a level line. Because its front and rear are exactly the same, you can save money by cutting the line exactly in half and using one half of it until it wears out. Then you can use the other half until it wears out. If you do this, use Dacron fishing line as backing to fill up your reel.

(Backing is line attached to the rear of your fly line or between the rear and the spool of your reel. It serves two purposes: one, to give you extra line in case you hook a fish strong enough to take all your fly line out and, two, to fill your reel so that you can retrieve line faster than if you had a partially full reel. Your backing should be stronger than your leader. Otherwise, you could lose your fly line if a strong fish snaps your backing.)

And, oh yes, speaking of leaders, you need several of those.

A leader separates your heavy fly line from your fly or other lure. In the beginning, you can use a length of level monofilament line for a leader. Later, you may want to buy knotless tapered leaders or tie your own knotted tapered ones. Tapered leaders have relatively heavy butt sections and then gradually become smaller until they reach the minimum size and strength you need for the fishing you are doing at the moment.

You will find instructions for tying tapered leaders in many books on fly fishing and in most leader-tying kits. The kits come with leader material of various sizes which you join together to make tapered leaders.

The length and strength of your leader will vary with the type of fishing you do. It is rarely necessary, however, to use a leader longer than your rod. Leaders and leader materials are usually listed in catalogs as Size 3x, Size 4x, and so on. But the strength of a 3x leader, for example, sometimes varies in test strength from manufacturer to manufacturer. For that reason, it is less confusing to buy leaders or leader materials that specify both their sizes (3x, 4x, and so on) and their strength (four-pound, six-pound, and so on).

Don Howell, a first-class mountain trout fisherman, likes knotted tapered leaders.

"I just think they roll your fly over better," he says.

Some other good fly rod anglers prefer knotless tapered leaders. This is especially true of anglers who do much of their fishing in water that has a lot of weeds. Knotted leaders have more of a tendency to snag aquatic grass.

If you use knotted leaders, you should frequently check your knots to be sure they are secure.

"That's where your weakness will be," Don Howell points out.

Some fly rod anglers who make their own leaders coat the knots with clear fingernail polish or glue such as Epoxy. This not only strengthens the knots but also makes them smoother so they will slip through the rod guides. It also helps keep the leaders from picking up grass.

Don Howell uses four-pound test leaders for most trout fishing but will switch to heavier leaders if he expects to catch larger than average trout. He will use smaller leaders if the water is unusually clear.

"But I seldom go below two-pound test," he says.

A four-pound test leader is also a good size to use for panfish such as bream.

Ten-pound test is a good size for smallmouth and largemouth bass. Seldom do you need anything heavier than a twelve-pound test leader, no matter where you fish in North Carolina fresh or brackish waters. Some people use a few inches of heavier monofilament as a tippet (the front end of the leader) if they expect to catch fish that can bite through lighter monofilament.

As you become more sophisticated and want to broaden your fly fishing horizons, you will need at least three different fly-fishing outfits to enable you to fish most of North Carolina's fresh and brackish waters.

Good fly anglers such as Bill Black, Don Howell, Bill Wilkerson, and John Baskervill generally agree that these are the three outfits that will enable you to fish for about any kind of fish you can reasonably expect to catch in sheltered waters from the mountains to the coast:

• A light rod. Anything from a six-and-a-half- to a seven-and-a-half-foot rod will do. The rod should be matched for a Number Four or Number Five line. A weight-forward line or a double-tapered line is ideal for this outfit. This is a good rod both for mountain trout in small streams and for bream and other panfish in lakes and farm ponds. A trout or big bream will give you a good fight on this outfit.

• An eight-and-half-foot rod matched for a Number Eight line and a reel that will take that size line. A floating bass bug or saltwater taper line is a good choice for this outfit. The eight-and-a-half-foot rod is good for smallmouth in both rivers and lakes and largemouth bass in about any kind of water that you will find in North Carolina. Under most conditions, this outfit will also handle just about any other fish you can readily catch in sheltered waters of North

Carolina. If you expect to catch larger fish such as striped bass on this outfit, add Dacron backing to your line.

• A heavy nine-foot rod and a heavy saltwater reel loaded with a Number Nine or Ten bass-bug or saltwater-tapered line and Dacron backing. I just about always carry a nine-foot rod in my boat and switch from my eight-and-a-half footer to the heavier rod when the wind blows hard.

"A nine-foot fly rod matched for a Number Nine or Ten line is a powerful fishing tool," says Bill Wilkerson. "It can handle about any reasonable-size fish, including bluefish, that you'll catch on a fly rod."

There is another reason for carrying both an eight-and-a-half footer and a heavier nine footer when you fish big lakes or vast Eastern North Carolina waters such as the North River or Alligator River. The nine-foot rod, although heavier than many people like to use for largemouth bass, serves as a spare if you should break your eight-and-a-half-foot rod while on a fishing trip.

I learned this lesson the hard way many years ago. I was fishing Currituck Sound on a late spring day with my son, Conrad, and guide Clarence Beasley. The first day, there were no clouds and little breeze. It was hot. We did not get a single strike that day.

That night, however, a light rain began to tick on the roof of Walnut Island Motel, where Conrad and I were staying. It continued to fall the next day, making it pleasant to fish in our lightweight rain suits. This was when Currituck was still one of the world's best places to fish for largemouth bass, and, for an hour or so, I caught bass on just about every cast with my eight-and-a-half-foot fly rod and a bass bug. Conrad, using a spinning rod, caught a fair number of bass but fewer than I caught on the fly rod.

Then, after I landed yet another bass, the tip of my rod broke. I didn't have a spare fly rod. So I switched to a spinning rod and a Tiny Torpedo and continued to catch bass but not nearly as many as I had with the fly rod. From that day on, I have carried a nine-foot rod along with my other rods when I fish big waters.

Besides, you may need a heavy rod rigged and ready to cast in the event that you should be lucky enough to happen upon a school of big bluefish or striped bass breaking the surface of the water.

By the way, rod builder Tom Kirkman likes to equip all his rods with fighting butts, no matter their weights and lengths. A fighting butt is an extension to a rod's reel seat. It is designed primarily to rest against your stomach when you fight big fish.

"It keeps the reel out of the dirt when you rest the butt on the ground to change flies or do something else," he says. "It also gives your rod balance when you rest it on boat seats or cross bars of a canoe."

Most fighting butts are made so that they can be removed if you wish and then quickly plugged back in if you should need to land a big fish.

If you like to build things, you can save money by buying a fly-rod kit and putting it together yourself. Making a simple rod that will catch fish is possible even for an amateur. It does require time and patience but is something to keep you out of mischief in the winter when it is too cold to fish.

Someday, you may also want to make your own bream and bass bugs and tie your own flies. Many local fly fishing clubs, fly fishing equipment stores and even some educational institutions offer fly tying courses. You also can find some very good books on the subject (see Appendix A).

When you become so addicted to fly fishing that you want to try every kind North Carolina has to offer, you'll need a boat. For cool-weather wading in smallmouth bass streams such as the New River in the mountains and for largemouth bass fishing in places such as Lake Mattamuskeet in Eastern North Carolina, you'll need chest waders. You could also use your chest waders for cool-weather trout fishing in smaller mountain streams, but hip boots are more suitable for that kind of fishing.

In warm weather, you don't even need waders or hip boots. You can "wade wet" or in shorts or old pants and tennis shoes. Many people who wade wet glue carpet to the bottoms of their shoes.That gives the shoes traction on the slippery rocks that clutter most North Carolina trout and smallmouth bass streams.

A wading staff also helps you to keep your balance when you are moving along a swift, boulder-strewn stream. You use the staff to probe the bottom of the stream in front of you as you pick your way over the moss-slick stones and through currents which are sometimes swift enough to knock you down if you are not careful. Bill Black and John Baskervill, two good fly rod fishermen, make their own wading staffs from rigid aluminum tubing.

To make a staff similar to those fashioned by Bill and John, you first cut a piece of tube long enough to act as a walking stick. You can cut it to a length that will suit your height. Sixty inches is a good length if you are six feet tall or taller. Use a shorter length down to about fifty inches if you are less than six feet tall. To one end of the aluminum tubing, attach a bicycle handlebar grip with a piece of cord in the shape of a lanyard. Insert a piece of wood dowel to the other end, or the end that touches the bottom of the stream (see photo). The lanyard allows you to carry the staff

Photo by Buck Paysour

Wading staff fashioned by author from aluminum tubing, wood dowel, bicycle handlebar grip and cord. A wading staff helps an angler keep balance in whitewater mountain streams.

around your neck or shoulder so that your hands are free to make casts when you stop to make a cast.

"A wading staff not only helps you keep your balance in a stream," says Bill Black, "but it comes in handy when you are crawling down a bank to get into the stream or trying to climb up a bank when you are getting out of a stream."

Probably more than any other kind of fishing, fly fishing offers something for almost every person's tastes.

You don't have to have a flawless casting technique to catch fish. In fact, some anglers who have less than perfect form consistently catch fish. But if style is important to you, then fly fishing offers that.

If you like to make things, fly fishing offers the chance for that. You can make your own rods, wading staffs, popping bugs and leaders and tie your own flies.

Fly fishing can even offer you the opportunity for the study of entomology (the study of insects) if you are interested in "matching the hatch" or choosing flies that imitate insects that make up the diet of mountain trout at any given time. Although matching the hatch is not as important in North Carolina fly fishing (see Chapter Nine and Appendix C) as in many other places, some North Carolina fly rod anglers nevertheless immerse themselves in the investigation of insect life and how it relates to what fish eat.

Then there is fly tying. Some anglers spend more time tying beautiful flies than they do fishing the flies. When done to perfection, fly tying is an art form. Some of the best-known fly tyers are women. But it is a hobby that men can also enjoy.

If you, like me, are clumsy and have big fingers and can't tie a beautiful fly every time, you can still create flies that will catch fish. Some good fly rod anglers are convinced that flies that don't precisely duplicate ones in the beautiful color plates of books sometimes catch more fish than the perfectly tied ones. Those that are poorly constructed often just look more buggy than those in books.

Speaking of books, fly fishing also appeals to many avid readers and intellectuals because no other method of fishing has given birth to so much good literature. So if you like to read good writing, fly fishing can offer you that too. I'm speaking here not of how-to books such as those listed in the appendix. I'm referring, rather, to literature such as Norman Maclean's *A River Runs Through It*, Harry Middleton's *On the Spine of Time*, and the fly fishing books by Robert Traver, among others.

If you are a nature lover, North Carolina fly fishing should entice you. The state has a variety of natural beauty ranging from high mountains to the solitude of the Coastal Plain. And fly fishing, better than any other kind of fishing, is a wonderful way to enjoy that great variety of beauty and to actually become a part of it.

Even though I did not take up fly rod fishing until relatively late in life, I became a fanatic when I finally did take it up. I still consider myself a neophyte as compared to many other anglers I know. So I sometimes practice on dry land. I do this by cutting off the barb of the hook on a fly or popping bug so it will not hang up. Then I attach the fly or bug onto the leader on a fly rod and stroll down to a park near my Greensboro home and cast toward clumps of grass, tree trunks, and other targets.

Some automobile and pickup truck drivers slow down and shake their heads in pity when they see me casting on waterless territory.

Some even stop and yell, "Catching anything?"

When I first started using the park as a practice field, I ignored those smart alecks. But then I hit upon the perfect answer to their taunts.

Now when somebody asks me how many I've caught, I try to look deranged—a feat that some of my friends probably think is not too difficult for me.

"Yeah!" I then shout. "You're the third one I've caught today!"

If you're not already hooked on North Carolina fly fishing, maybe I can snare you in the pages that follow.

Photo by Lynn Hey

Retired lawyer G. Neil
Daniels, for whom the
G. Neil fly is named.

The G. Neil fly.

Photo by Leger Meyland

Chapter Two

Small Sunfish: Good Teachers

Bob Suggs and his cousin, Ted Ray, and I have driven from Greensboro to Lumberton to fish the Lumber River for robin redbreast.

Ted and Bob are Lumberton natives who fished and hunted on the Lumber River when they were boys. But they have not been back on the river in some forty years.

For a long time, they have lived in Greensboro where Bob is a lawyer. Ted commutes from Greensboro to Winston-Salem where he is in the insurance business.

At Lumberton, before daylight, we meet a fisherman with the fitting name of Jim Bass. Jim has agreed to be our guide for a day and a half of fishing. He is a former firefighter who was disabled when he fell through the floor of a burning mobile home while searching for two children who were reported to be inside but were not.

Jim suggests that we put our boats in the river at Lumberton. After we launch, he climbs into Ted's boat. Bob fishes with me in my boat.

We move up the river only about fifty feet when I conclude that this is going to be some of the most fascinating fishing I have ever done—no matter how good or bad the fishing.

The narrow blackwater river is beautiful. Although it is summer, moss-bearded cypress trees shade the stream, and the air is comfortably cool. Something else makes this reach of water intriguing. We will be fishing right in town most of the day, yet you would not know that from what you see on the river's west shore. On that side, there is usually little but open countryside.

On the other side, the city reaches down almost to the water. Even so, the river is uncrowded and serene and only our ears tell us we are in a city.

Even though it is a weekday, the First Baptist Church's bells toll every thirty minutes or so. We also hear the roar of trucks, the honking of car horns, the rumble of trains, the screaming sirens of ambulances on the way to the hospital. These noises mingle with the sounds of nature: the mournful call of doves, the sigh of the river, the bob-bob-white of quails.

At one stretch of the river, Bob and I hear the banging of hammers. As we drift past the hammering, carpenters working on the roof of a house yell "redbreast, redbreast, redbreast" at us.

The carpenters correctly assume that we are angling, as do most people who journey over this section of the river, for the fish that gets its name from its brilliant red underside.

We move on past the workmen.

Occasionally a one-man boat drifts past us. These boats, made especially for streams like this, look so small and sit so low in the water you would think the slightest wave would swamp them. But they are very stable. Occupants fit their bodies in the boats by half sitting and half reclining, much like the position a person assumes while reading in bed, propped up on a pillow. The boats are propelled with electric trolling motors or with hand-held oars not much larger than Ping-Pong paddles.

Kingfishers, my favorite birds, dart to and fro over the water.

Muskrats glide across the river, leaving bright trails on the dark water.

"Look over there," Bob says, as we pass an undercut bank.

A muskrat is in a hole peering out at us from behind some exposed tree roots. I reach for my camera, but before I can focus, the animal slides into the water and, with a flick of its tail, disappears.

We catch some redbreast, including a few that hit my fly rod popper.

But somehow, catching fish is secondary to just being here.

One thing that makes the trip so pleasant is listening to Bob, Ted, and Jim talk about the river and the town that lies beside it. Bob and Ted remember a blacksmith shop where they used to acquire horseshoes.

"Those were really great horseshoes to pitch," Bob says.

Bob and Ted remember the former textile mill that we can see from one spot on the river. It is now just an abandoned building. The two men also remember the theater where they once watched cowboy movies. They remember other institutions of their youth. Most of all, they remember the river and the adventures the river provided.

As we take our boats out of the water after our final half day of fishing, I realize that you can go home again. Especially when home is as beautiful and as fascinating as the Lumber River.

You don't have to drive as far as we did that day to catch robin redbreast or other small sunfish, also known as panfish, on a fly rod. No matter where you live in North Carolina, you will find them not much more than a good double haul cast away. And, if you are just beginning to fly fish, small sunfish can teach you some valuable lessons. Fishing for them is the best way to learn to fly fish.

If you fish even occasionally, you know there are no sure things about the sport. You can catch plenty of fish one day and then go back to the very same place the next day and fish with the same tackle without getting even a sniff from a fish. Fish will tear up a certain fly or other artificial lure or natural bait for an hour, then turn up their noses at it the next hour. One person can fish a particular fly or other lure or other bait and catch fish after fish on it while another person using the same lure, and fishing it in what looks like the exact same way, can not get a single strike.

Yet I have found a way to use a fly rod to win a bet—on most days, at least.

Here is how I do it:

When my partner and I are fishing in fresh or brackish water for relatively big fish—such as largemouth bass—and haven't caught a fish in a long time, I set the trap.

"Bet you fifty cents I catch a fish in the next ten minutes," I say.

I am careful not to disclose what species I plan to catch, what size it will be, or how I plan to catch it.

Most of the time, my partner—if he is one who has not fallen for the trick before—will take me up on the bet.

That's when I reach for my seven-foot ultralight fly rod. If the water is relatively cool or relatively hot, I tie on a sinking fly, usually a Number Eight or Number Ten Woolly Worm. If the water is moderately warm, I tie on a Number Six or Number Eight popping bug and start casting.

More times than not, I'll catch a bluegill bream, a pumpkinseed, a robin redbreast or other small sunfish within the specified ten minutes. Many times, depending on where my partner and I are fishing, the fish will be no larger than two or three inches long. But it'll be a fish and, if you recall, that's all I wagered I would catch.

That's one thing I admire about sunfish: you can just about always catch them on a fly rod. In some North Carolina waters, bream and their sunfish relatives grow to be surprisingly large, and they are scrappy on a light fly rod. (Although the sunfish family includes larger fish such as smallmouth and largemouth bass, in this chapter "sunfish" refers only to the smaller members of the family such as bluegill bream and robin redbreast and other similar panfish.)

Because sunfish are so easy to catch, they are very good teachers.

"Panfishing is the absolute best way to learn to use a fly rod," says Bill Wilkerson. "Panfishing is the quickest way of learning the rhythm that is required of fly casting."

Don Howell agrees.

"It's one of the best ways to learn trout fishing," he says. "You develop the timing and technique it takes to use a fly rod."

Most people probably think of trout when they think of fly fishing, but a trout stream is the worst place for a beginner to learn to fly fish, especially in most of North Carolina. The majority of the state's trout streams are small and have thick underbrush and other vegetation along their banks. Trees often grow over the streams like umbrellas. Fortunately, you often do not have to make long casts (see Chapters Eight and Nine) to catch trout in North Carolina. But when you do need to cast twenty feet or so beyond you, you often have to roll cast or make your back casts low to the water—techniques you can master while fishing elsewhere for small sunfish.

"When you fish for bream, you can usually find places on farm ponds (see Chapter Sixteen) and other sunfish waters where there are no obstructions behind you to foul your back cast," Bill Wilkerson says.

Fishing for bream and other small sunfish is also a good way for a beginning fly rodder to learn to cast accurately. To catch trout and bass and many other species of larger fish on a fly rod, you often have to put your fly close to a fishy-looking spot or close to where you have seen a swirl or other sign of a fish.

"You have to be an extremely good caster to catch trout," says Don Howell. "That doesn't mean coming close. Close doesn't count. It's not like pitching horseshoes."

There is another reason why fishing for sunfish is a good way to learn to use a fly rod, Bill Wilkerson says.

"It is not as tiring as fishing for trout," he says. "You don't have to wade and climb over rocks all day. So you can concentrate on learning to use the fly rod."

And that's not all.

"Bream fishing is a good way to learn how to set your hook and to play a fish," Bill Wilkerson says. "Then, when you go trout fishing, you have at least a forty percent better chance of being able to hook, play and land a fish."

The beginning fly rod angler has yet another reason to fish for small sunfish. Sunfish will hit just about any fly, wet or dry, that North Carolina mountain trout (see Chapters Seven, Eight and Nine) will take. So you can buy a set of large or medium-sized wet and dry flies, use them for sunfish until you learn to use a fly rod reasonably well, then use the same flies to fish for mountain trout.

Sunfish have other characteristics that make them appealing to the beginning fly rod angler. You will find sunfish near your home, no matter where you live in North Carolina. They live in waters as diverse as the deep mountain lakes of Western North Carolina and the vast and shallow fresh-and-brackish water sounds and rivers of Eastern North Carolina—and about everywhere in between.

In Eastern North Carolina, you can catch sunfish on a fly rod in the freshwater or brackish-water portions of Alligator River, Cashie River, Chowan River, North River, Pamlico River, Perquimans River, Pungo River, Roanoke River, White Oak River, and just about every other river or creek that flows into the Pamlico or Albemarle Sounds or into the ocean. In fact, pumpkinseed bream and some other small sunfish tolerate higher levels of salinity than do largemouth bass and some other freshwater species. But freshwater streams or streams that are only slightly brackish are the best places to catch sunfish in Eastern North Carolina.

Moving inland, you can catch sunfish on a fly rod in the populous Piedmont. I have used a fly rod to catch sunfish after sunfish on lakes such as Wylie and Norman near Charlotte, the state's largest city; on High Rock near Lexington and Salisbury; on Lake Hickory near Hickory and Statesville; on Mountain Island near Gastonia and Charlotte; on Gaston and Kerr (Buggs Island) near Durham and Raleigh; on a number of city water supply lakes; and every other large North Carolina Piedmont lake I have fished.

Every North Carolina city water supply lake that is open to public fishing holds panfish that even a beginning fly rod angler can often catch.

I live near the center of Greensboro but occasionally see people fishing for sunfish in a stream that flows through a park near my home. I have never fished it myself, though.

41

The creek is polluted, and I just don't think I would enjoy fishing it.

Western North Carolina mountain lakes such as Chatuge, Cheoah, Fontana, Hiwassee, Nantahala, and Santeetlah have some big bream and other sunfish.

Most North Carolina farm ponds have sunfish. In fact, farm ponds and other private lakes are among the best places to catch big bluegill bream. A friend of mine, John Ellison, Sr., owns a Piedmont lake (see Chapter Sixteen) where we often catch a string of bluegill and redear "shell-cracker" bream that average a pound or more each on our fly rods and small popping bugs or sinking flies.

Another friend, the late Claibourne Darden, owned several Guilford County lakes where we often caught large bream. The biggest shellcracker bream I ever caught came from one of Claibourne's lakes. I confess that I caught it on an ultralight spinning rig—not a fly rod. It weighed a pound and fourteen ounces. I later learned it would have made the national outdoor magazines as one of the largest caught that year on four-pound-test line. But I once more missed my moment in the national spotlight. Not knowing that the bream would have given me my fifteen minutes of fame, we ate the fish instead of having it weighed on certified scales in front of witnesses.

For some reason, sunfish on many larger North Carolina lakes and rivers are often smaller than those found in farm ponds. You can, nevertheless, catch some nice sunfish on larger waters.

The biggest bluegill bream I have ever seen anybody catch on a fly rod was caught on Currituck Sound. Roger Soles, who was fishing for bass, caught it. As he usually does, Roger was using a small bass bug, about a Number Six. We did not weigh the bream. But take my word for it. It was larger than many of the bass we caught on that trip.

Like Roger, John Baskervill often fishes a popper that John describes as "too small for bass and too big for bream."

"Sometimes both bass and bream will hit it," John says. "If you get a bream on it, it's usually a pretty good one because it takes a pretty good one to swallow it."

Furthermore, John often catches bass on the same bug.

"Usually the bass are small, but occasionally, you'll get a good one on it," he says.

John describes this as "shotgun fishing."

As with other types of fishing, most fly rod anglers think the most thrilling way of catching panfish is on top of the water. The very best time to do this is when the fish are bedding. Bream and their relatives usually commence spawning in the spring when the water temperature is about seventy degrees Fahrenheit. Most sunfish spawn in shallow water, and if you drop a floating bug or dry fly near a bed, a fish will usually whack it. A big bream will strike a topwater offering with a swirl, making a loud gulping or sucking sound. Then it will put a bend in your ultralight fly rod that will make you respect it. It darts in tight circles, at right angles to the line.

The spawning season is about the only time of the year when you can catch shellcrackers on top of the water. Even then, however, you won't do it very often. The rest of the year, shellcrackers will hardly ever hit anything except a sinking fly or other underwater lure.

Shellcrackers have tile-like plates in their mouths for crushing mollusks and other hard organisms that make up their favorite food. Hence the name "shellcracker."

When the water is clear, it is easy to spot bream beds. The beds look like miniature moon craters. Bluegills, especially, bed several times during spring and early summer. Some knowledgeable anglers believe that bluegill bed on each full moon through the warm months. You can, believe it or not, sometimes smell bream beds. A musky odor hovers over the water close to them.

Sunfish are prolific spawners. So there is nothing immoral or unsportsmanlike about catching them on their beds. If you are squeamish about doing this, however, you can still catch them on top without fishing beds. Sunfish clobber topwater offerings after they come off their beds and continue to do so until the water gets hot. Even in the summer, they will frequently take dry flies, floating rubber spiders, and cork poppers all day long—especially on cloudy days. But the best times to use topwater flies and similar things in the summer is early in the morning and late in the afternoon. Sunfish will also strike topwater offerings in the fall before the water gets too cold.

As do most other fish, sunfish usually prefer to hang around cover. On occasion, however, you will catch them in open water. When they are in open water, they usually prefer sinking flies, yet will, on occasion, hit on top even then.

During both hot and cold weather, however, you usually have to fish under the water. I confess that when sunfish are far below the surface, I switch to a spinning rod. To me, it is just too awkward and too much work to try to use a deep sinking fly line, especially on a light rod of the type I prefer to use for small fish.

When you use a floating line and a sinking fly, it's almost as much fun to catch bream and other small sunfish under water as it is to catch them on top. You keep a sharp lookout on your line. Then, when it spurts across the water signalling a strike, you set your hook—much as you do when fishing nymphs and other wet flies for trout. If you are my age or older and your eyes aren't as sharp as they once were, you can attach a "strike indicator" to your line. The strike indicator helps you to see movements of your line. Later, when you fish for mountain trout with nymphs or other sinking flies, you can use the same strike indicator to help you detect a pick-up.

The indicator serves the same purpose that a float serves when you fish with a pole. You usually don't need an indicator to help you recognize a hit when a big bream hits your sinking fly, however. The strike will be so hard, it feels as if it will yank your light rod from your hands.

Whether you fish on top or under the water, panfish seem to prefer a fly fished slow most of the time, especially if you are fishing in relatively shallow and calm water. Many of your strikes will come when your floating fly or bug is sitting still. If the water is fairly rough or deep, or both, you may have to make your floating fly or bug dance and gurgle to get the attention of your quarry. On days when fishing is slow, do both. Let your dry fly or floating bug sit still for a few seconds after the cast. Then twitch it or make it dart across the surface. Then let it sit again and then make it spurt again.

If you are using a nymph or other wet (sinking) fly, let it sit still after it has fallen as far as it can, then make it dart or wiggle under the water. In other words, try to make it appear erratic. There is hardly a wrong way of fishing a bug or fly for sunfish.

When you can't coax sunfish into hitting a topwater fly or bug, almost any fly that sinks will catch them in North Carolina. But some favorites include Woolly Worms and other nymphs, Black Ants and small spinner flies. Some of the best fly fishermen I know—including Bill Black, Roger Soles, John Ellison, and Dr. John Gray Hunter—swear by a sinking fly called the "G. Neil." It is slightly weighted and looks (see Chapter Seven) much like a Woolly Worm except that the hackle is trimmed close, whereas the regular Woolly Worm has a hackle that is a little more bushy. The

G. Neil is tied by Don Howell of Brevard and is named for Greensboro angler G. Neil Daniels. It evolved from a fly that an Indian guide gave Neil, who was fishing in northern Canada at the time.

"It was a good fly," Neil recalls. "But I thought it did not sink fast enough."

So he brought it back home and sent it to brothers Don and Dwight Howell, nationally known fly tiers, and asked them to tie a similar fly but weight it slightly. That's what they did.

Don continued to tie the G. Neil after Dwight died, and it is now popular with anglers who fish for bream and other sunfish, especially in the North Carolina Piedmont. It is also well-known in North Carolina as a good trout fly. Neil is one of the few people I know who has a fly named for him.

Don Howell, himself, ties two flies that people began calling "Don's Stone Fly" and "Don's Pet" in his honor.

Vince Davis also comes close to having a fly named for him. He designed and ties a fly (see Chapter Nine) that is dubbed the "In-Vince-A-Beetle."

Don's Stone Fly was named for its designer, fly fisherman Don Howell.

Photo by Leger Meyland

I envy them all. I would rather have a fly named for me than to have a road, a skyscraper, or a bridge named for me.

Here are some of the more important members of the small sunfish family that can be caught on a fly rod in most areas of North Carolina:

• Bluegill bream. Perhaps the most popular of sunfishes. Its color varies depending on the time of the year it is caught and the characteristics of the water it occupies. But the bluegill, especially a larger one, is most often copper tinted. The female usually has a reddish, yellow, or orange breast. The male is more of a solid copper color. The gill covers of both the male and female are usually dark blue, fringed with powder blue. That's where the fish gets the name "bluegill."

The bluegill will readily take almost any kind of small floating or sinking fly or popper. The fish are delicious, especially when deep fried.

• Redear or shellcracker bream. Looks much like a blue-gill but has red fringes on its gill cover. Hence the name "redear"—"fish with red ears." The shellcracker is not as easy to catch on artificial lures as is the bluegill, but it will take many types of sinking flies fished close to the bottom or on the bottom. Will hit a topwater lure or fly only on rare occasions.

The redear is not quite as good to eat as is the bluegill. But what is?

• Pumpkinseed bream. It has a reddish or orange fringe on its gill flaps and looks a little like the shellcracker but is smaller and more colorful. It is so bright, it seems as if it has absorbed the brilliance of a sunrise or sunset. It will hit both floating and sinking flies. I have caught them on a fly rod in Eastern North Carolina brackish water that was too salty for most other freshwater fish.

Photo by Buck Paysour

One-man boat of the type used on blackwater rivers to fish for
robin redbreast.

• Redbreast. Is often called "robin" because of its red underside. Has long gill flap. Will take just about any kind of fly or popper. Inhabits many kinds of water but prefers moving, blackwater rivers. The Black, Lumber and Waccamaw Rivers and similar streams in North Carolina are especially well known for redbreast.

• Longear sunfish. Its gill cover is long but, despite its name, it is not as long as the robin redbreast's gill cover. Although the longear ("fish with long ears") is among the smallest of the sunfish, it often feeds on top, making it a good fish to catch on a fly rod.

• Green sunfish. It is olive colored, as its name suggests, and has a reddish fringe on gill cover. It does not grow as large as the bluegill but is a sporty fish and good to eat. Will hit almost any kind of fly or popper.

Yes, the bream and its sunfish relatives are good species to fish for if you are a novice fly rod angler. But you don't have to be a novice to enjoy catching sunfish. They offer a lifetime of enjoyment even for the veteran fly rod angler.

Photo by Buck Paysour

Bill Smith, left, a fishing guide, nets a Coastal Plain largemouth bass caught by Roger Soles.

Chapter Three

Coastal Plain Largemouth

I remember when I first began to have doubts about large-mouth bass tournaments and so-called "professional bass anglers." It was during a fishing seminar conducted by John Powell, then a celebrated "professional" bass tournament fisherman. The seminar was held at the Greensboro Coliseum.

Powell extolled the advantages of using heavy baitcasting equipment and landing a hooked bass as quickly as possible.

"If you want to play with the fish," he told his worshipful audience, "do it after you get him in the boat!"

Many of his listeners laughed. I wanted to weep.

If you agree with Powell's philosophy, don't even think about fishing with a fly rod for bass. You won't enjoy it. It will be too sporting for you. It is also often more challenging than other methods of bass fishing.

"I think it is even harder to catch bass on fly rod than it is to catch mountain trout on a fly rod," says John Baskervill, the best all-around fly fisherman I know.

Vince Davis of Lewisville, a very good fly fisherman, agrees.

"At least that's been my experience," he says. "I can go out and catch trout most any day. That's not true of bass, even though I have had some great days fishing for largemouth bass."

It makes me feel better about my fly fishing when I hear fly rod anglers that I admire say that, because I have caught hundreds upon hundreds of largemouth bass on a fly rod. I have caught some of them when conditions were horrible— when the wind was blowing a gale, for example. Yet I still do not have a lot of confidence in my mountain-trout fishing skills.

And while one might debate which kind of fishing is the most difficult, the fly rod can often be a potent instrument for catching largemouth bass. I have seen Roger Soles, the best largemouth-bass fly rod fisherman I have ever fished with, catch and release as many as a hundred bass a day. I, myself, since I learned to use a fly rod, have caught limits of bass on fly tackle many more times than I have caught limits on spinning or baitcasting outfits. This, admittedly, may be because I use the fly rod more often than I use baitcasting equipment. Still, there are circumstances when the fly rod will outfish other types of equipment.

In Eastern North Carolina, especially, bass will sometimes turn up their noses at everything except a fly rod popping bug. A small bass I caught on Currituck Sound was an example of that.

I was fishing with Wallace O'Neal, my friend and favorite fishing guide, and Curtis Youngblood, also a good friend. The water was low, and we were fishing a pond that was connected to the sound by an inlet. We were casting to pockets between the marsh and the aquatic grass that occupied much of the water. I caught a fair number of bass on the fly rod, and Curtis picked up one now and then on his spinning outfit and a three-eighths-ounce Jitterbug lure. Then I spotted an interesting looking hole in the grass in the middle of the pond and suggested to Mr. O'Neal that we fish it.

"I've already seen it," Mr. O'Neal replied. "I thought we would move out there after we fish this stretch of marsh."

When Mr. O'Neal was satisfied that we had caught all the fish we were going to catch along the marsh, he poled the boat to within casting distance of the hole.

Curtis cast his Jitterbug to the right side of the hole, which was about the size of a Volkswagen beetle. I was using my home-made popping bug, which was only about two inches long measured from the eye of the hook to the rear of the feathers. I cast to the left side of the hole. The bug landed about six feet from Curtis's much larger Jitterbug.

The grass just a few inches from the Jitterbug quivered. Then a wake, like the trail of a toy motor boat, emerged from the grass. The wake was obviously made by a bass.

The fish almost accidentally bumped into Curtis's Jitterbug. But it ignored the lure as it headed straight to my popping bug on the other side of the hole!

"Look at him coming!" I said as the bass streaked across the water. "Look at him coming!"

When the fish reached the other side of the clearing, it turned over, flashing a white belly in the clear water, and nailed my bug.

Curtis, after uttering a few choice cuss words, slammed down his rod with such force that it is a wonder he did not shatter it. It was the first and last time I ever heard Curtis, usually a gentleman, use profanity. Although the bass that hit my bug was small, I had more fun catching it than any other except the first one I caught on a fly rod.

To paraphrase something my fishing buddy Wilt Browning once said about pets, God must have had bass fly rod anglers in mind when He created Eastern North Carolina. Certainly, much of the water that God brought forth in that part of the state is perfect for fly fishing for bass. It is mostly shallow so you don't have to fish deep, something many fly rod anglers would just as soon not have to do. Because the water is so shallow, topwater lures—especially fly rod lures—are deadly in Eastern North Carolina for much of the year.

One reason a bass fly, whether sinking or floating, is often so effective in shallow water of Eastern North Carolina is because it does not make a heavy splash when it hits the water as does a spinning of baitcasting lure. Noises in shallow water are more apt to spook fish than noises in deep water.

"A bass bug hits the water more softly," Roger Soles says. "It sounds more life-like."

That's why Roger, when he fly fishes Eastern North Carolina waters, generally uses a smaller bug than the size fished by many other fly rod anglers.

Claibourne Darden, another very good fisherman, also used smaller bugs. I often fish a little larger bug. When I fished with Claibourne on days when he caught bass and I had not caught anything for a while, he would throw me one of his small popping bugs and insist that I use it. Often, it changed my luck.

James A. King, Sr., a long-time fly rod fisherman, thought the relative smallness and lightness of bass bugs were some of the reasons bass often hit the bugs when they would scorn spinning and baitcasting lures.

"The bass bug is so small, it's kind of like a hors d'oeuvre to them," he said. "They will often hit it even when they are not hungry."

Aubrey Edwards, Mr. King's fishing buddy, agreed. He recalled that he and Mr. King often caught bass on popping bugs even when the bass were so full of minnows that they could not possibly be very hungry.

Of course, these things can sometimes apply to shallow water in other parts of North Carolina, but they are more true of Eastern North Carolina than anywhere else in the state.

There is, perhaps, still another reason why Eastern North Carolina is so good for fly rod fishing. Much of the area's water holds abundant growths of aquatic weeds. That's both a blessing and a curse. It can be a blessing for the fly rod angler but is a curse for anglers using other kinds of equipment.

Why? If you are a reasonably good fly caster, you can flip a fly rod bug or streamer into a small clearing in the grass and work it across the clearing. If you don't get a hit, you simply pick up the fly before it reaches grass on the other side and flip it to another hole—all without it touching grass.

If you use a spinning or baitcasting outfit, you can cast into the clear spot in the grass and work your lure from one side of the hole to the other without any problem. Then, however, you have to retrieve your lure across the grass where it usually becomes entangled—often even if the lure is "weedless." Then you are compelled to clean the grass from your lure before you make another cast.

Also, bass bugs are so light that they don't get hung up, even in grass, as much as do heavy lures. I make bass bugs that I plan to use in Eastern North Carolina semi-weedless by tying a loop of monofilament line between the eye and shank of the hook (see photo). The monofilament should be rigid enough to ride over weeds but flexible enough so that it can be bent by pressure from a fish's strike. Some people use other things, such as a short piece of stiff monofilament glued into the body of the bug with the end protruding down in front of the point of the hook. This works like the weedguard on a Johnson weedless spoon. I personally find the loop easier to fashion, especially when you are making your bugs from scratch. I also think it works better because it protects the entire hook. But you can throw a bug that is equipped with either of these kinds of weedguards right into the weeds and hold your rod high to crawl the bug across the weeds, usually without hanging.

I recall one trip to Eastern North Carolina when this technique paid off for my son, John, and me. We had fished Smith and Scranton Creeks off the Pungo River with Claibourne Darden and John Peterson without catching anything. Late in the afternoon, John and I stopped at a large grass bed next to the boat landing on Scranton Creek. We cast my homemade weedless popping bugs into the grass and caught a number of bass. All were small, but all hit hard. It was fun watching the bass swirl several times at our bugs before nailing them. The grass was so thick, we had to dig several of the hooked bass out with a landing net.

You can also fish lily pads by holding your rod tip high and retrieving your semi-weedless bug across the pads. Sometimes, bass will blast holes in the pads to get to a bug. At other times, bass will strike just as the bug clears the pads and falls into open water. Apparently, the bass follow your bug out of the lily pads before hitting it.

Even underwater fly rod lures, such as streamers, come through weeds better than do the heavier spinning and bait-casting lures. Streamers such as Chico Bendbacks, whose hooks ride up, are especially good in the grass of Eastern North Carolina—and in grass and bushes anywhere else for that matter.

56

John Baskervill often uses only three fly rod lures for bass whether he fishes in Eastern North Carolina or elsewhere: a popping bug, a Clouser Minnow, and a spinner fly (see photos). The Clouser Minnow is a weighted streamer. The spinner fly is a small spinner trailed by a fly.

"If I had to choose just two flies for Eastern North Carolina," John says, "I would chose a popping bug and a Clouser."

About any streamer that imitates minnows will often take bass. So will anything that imitates small eels.

John always uses a floating line in Eastern North Carolina, and usually elsewhere for that matter, whether he is fishing topwater or underwater offerings. When it comes to fishing on the surface, he hardly ever uses anything other than cork bugs.

"I like the Peck's Popper that goes back to our childhood," he says. "They still make them and they are as good as any there are."

John will use a floating hair bug only occasionally.

When I use a deer hair bug, it seems to work better when it gets wet enough so that most of it is under the water. It then creates an interesting commotion on the surface as you twitch it.

Young Alan Howell, a good fly rod fisherman and skilled fly tyer, has an interesting theory about why fish often prefer a water-logged bug. He believes fish can see a bug better when most of it is under water than when only the bottom is visible to the fish. That makes sense. I wonder also if a soggy hair bug doesn't look more like a real mouse or some other small animal that is swimming across the water.

John Baskervill, of course, is right when he says that a cork bug is usually as effective as a hair bug or even more effective. But on rare occasions, in Eastern North Carolina

Semi-weedless bug made by author bears the teeth marks of many bass. The loop of monofilament enables cork bug to crawl over weeds, lily pads and other obstructions.

Photo by Buck Paysour

These may be the only flies needed to catch a variety of fish in brackish water. They are, from left to right, popper, spinner fly, and Clouser Minnow.

and elsewhere, I have caught fish on hair bugs when I couldn't get even a sniff on a cork bug.

I especially remember one time when bass showed a conspicuous preference for something other than cork bugs. It was on a spring day not long after I first learned to use a fly rod. Bill Keys and I had fished Currituck Sound for several hours without having even one bass swirl at our cork bugs. Just to have something to do, I tied a big dry salmon fly to the end of my leader. After only a few casts, a bass boiled up and nailed the fly. I thought that was a fluke but kept casting the salmon fly. After a few minutes, I caught another bass. Then another and another.

Bill, a good fly fisherman, was still not having any luck with his cork bug. Nor did his kit contain anything similar to my fly. I rummaged through my fly box and found another dry salmon fly and handed it to Bill. He joined me in catching bass.

I still don't know why I had those salmon flies. I only fished for salmon one time and that was when I was in the Army, many years before I learned to use a fly rod.

When I returned home from Currituck Sound after Bill Keys and I caught those bass on those salmon flies, I got out my Orvis catalog (see Appendix B) to see if I could find the name of the flies. They were "Bombers."

Some very good places to fish for bass with a fly rod in Eastern North Carolina include the Alligator River, Big Flatty Creek and Little Flatty Creek, Chowan River, Colington Creek, Little River, Neuse River, North River, Pamlico River, Perquimans River, Pungo River, Roanoke River, White Oak River, and about any of the tributaries of those rivers.

Generally speaking, the best places to fish for bass in Eastern North Carolina rivers and their tributaries are in the upstream portions—areas where the salt content is not too high.

Bass thrive in waters where there is a moderate amount of salt. You can catch largemouth bass in Eastern North Carolina waters when you can taste just a hint of salt when you put your fly line in your mouth to help control the line after hooking fish.

But bass dislike large amounts of salt, and the quality of bass fishing in much of Eastern North Carolina varies with the amount of rain that falls in upstate North Carolina. During drought years, there is not enough flow of fresh water to keep large amounts of salt from seeping into Eastern North Carolina creeks, rivers and sounds.

Some people think that too much salt ruined Currituck Sound, once one of the best places in the world to fish for largemouth bass. Others believe, however, that high salinity levels are not the only reason for the demise of Currituck bass fishing. They think that development and agriculture runoff and other pollution have added to the sound's problems.

I dream of the day when Currituck bass fishing will once again be as good as it was during the twenty or so years that I fished it. There were not many days when I did not catch at least my limit of bass there. And on most days, I caught them on a fly rod.

The Pungo and Pamlico Rivers and their tributaries and other streams that flow into the Pamlico Sound are especially susceptible to becoming more brackish than largemouth bass enjoy. Even then, however, a fly fishing trip to these waters can be fruitful, for you could catch saltwater species (see Chapters Ten and Fourteen).

Sometimes, you can catch both freshwater fish and some species of saltwater fish in the same waters. Much of the water is often slightly brackish, which means it is fresh enough to hold many species of freshwater fish but still salty enough to accommodate some species of saltwater fish.

One fall day, Curtis Youngblood and I saw a tarpon leap from the water on Pungo Creek. The tarpon was playing where James A. King, Sr., Aubrey Edwards and I had caught our limits of largemouth bass on fly rods the day before and Curtis had caught some on a spinning outfit and a Jitterbug lure.

If you want to fly fish for freshwater fish exclusively in Eastern North Carolina, you can do it by fishing only the upper reaches of the rivers and creeks. Then, if you tire of fishing for freshwater fish and want to try your hand at fly fishing for saltwater fish, you can move to the lower reaches of the stream. The White Oak River, which empties into Bogue Sound near Swansboro, is a great place to do this. You can catch largemouth bass on a fly rod in upstream portions of the upper reaches of the river near Maysville and speckled sea trout on a fly rod while fishing below the bridge at Stella (see Chapters Ten and Fourteen).

Once, I fished the upper reaches of the White Oak River with Bill Black, John Peterson and Harry Gianaris. We were impressed with how hard the largemouth bass fought. The White Oak is one of the few places in North Carolina where you can catch largemouth bass in waters that are affected by a lunar tide. That could be one reason the bass are so strong; they must battle the ebb and flow of the river every day of their lives. Other Eastern North Carolina largemouth bass waters have wind tides but no moon tides. All Eastern North Carolina largemouth bass fight harder than do bass in most other North Carolina waters, but fish on the White Oak fight even harder.

61

One reason I enjoy fishing Eastern North Carolina with a fly rod, or any other type of gear for that matter, is that it is such a charming area to visit even when fishing is poor. Eastern North Carolinians are hospitable and know how to enjoy life. The barbecue and seafood are among the world's finest.

Furthermore, much of Eastern North Carolina is still unspoiled and uncrowded. Wildlife abounds. I see deer on almost every fishing trip I make to the area. In some places, you might even see an alligator with only half of its head sticking out of the water, looking for all the world like Pogo. If you are real lucky, you could spot a bald eagle. In the fall, Canada geese and mallards fill the air.

You may think I am weird for saying this, but I even enjoy seeing poisonous cottonmouth water moccasins in Eastern North Carolina, the only place in the state where they live. While fishing Currituck Sound one September day, I saw hundreds of them, and I see at least one or two almost every time I fish Eastern North Carolina during the spring, summer or fall.

An occasional bear will make an appearance. This happened once when I fished Eastern North Carolina with Jerry Bledsoe, Ed Hardin, Gary McCann, Wilt Browning, Wilt's son, Ken, and my two sons, John and Conrad.

We fished the Alligator River one day, and Jerry and I quit early to return to Belhaven to buy food for a dinner Jerry planned to cook at Conrad's Belhaven home. The others remained behind to fish a while longer.

When the others returned to Conrad's home, Wilt said, "Guess what Gary and I saw? We saw a bear swimming across the river."

I believed him because I had recently read in the Belhaven paper that a highway patrolman's wife had accidentally

Photo by Buck Paysour

Cottonmouth water moccasins are frequently encountered while fishing Eastern North Carolina waters.

struck and killed a bear as she drove her car along the highway near Belhaven. My confidence in Wilt and Gary's veracity was further corroborated when Conrad called me less than a week later.

"You won't believe what happened today," he said. "A big bear lumbered across my back yard and then down the street. People came out of their houses to look, and the bear became frightened and climbed a tree. Game protectors came and shot the bear with a tranquilizer dart. The bear dozed off and fell out of the tree. When he hit the ground, he grunted and woke up and started to stumble down the street again. The game protectors shot him again, and he fell asleep again, this time more soundly. The game protectors put him in the back of their truck and carried him out into the woods and released him."

Conrad's home is just several blocks away from his law office in downtown Belhaven. The Belhaven newspaper published photographs of the bear.

Eastern North Carolina is such a pleasure to visit that I don't even remember how many fish I caught on some of my most memorable trips to the area. But I do remember the little fawn lying in the marsh, the ospreys rising and falling on invisible thermal columns high overhead, the raccoon breaking open a clam shell on a rock, the big alligator lying beside the water, the beaver leaving a trail of gold as it swims across the creek in the dying sunlight....

Chapter Four

Inland Largemouth Bass

The bass fly rod is not as popular on the big lakes of Piedmont North Carolina or on the deep mountain lakes of Western North Carolina as it is in Eastern North Carolina. There's a good reason for that. It is more difficult to catch bass on a fly rod in the deeper waters of inland North Carolina than it is in the shallow waters of Eastern North Carolina.

Yet a fly rod angler can sometimes enjoy some fine largemouth bass fishing in inland North Carolina.

It is a fine cloudless day in early October, and the breezes are mellow. Bill Jerome, a neighbor, and I have driven the hundred miles from our Greensboro homes to Kerr (Buggs Island) Lake, a large reservoir that straddles the Virginia-North Carolina state line. It is about 8:30 A.M. when we launch our boat at Nutbush Landing on the southwest side of the lake. I pick up my eight-and-a-half-foot fly rod and cast a popping bug against some willows. Nothing happens.

I next cast to a stump. Again nothing. I cast and cast and cast. Still nothing happens; all morning long, not even a bream pecks at the counterfeit bug. Bill, using a spinning rod, also fishes hard but without success. The sun climbs higher in the cerulean sky. We do not get a single strike all morning. At noon when I steer the boat into a cove, I select a clearing in the trees that looks as if it would be a pleasant place to eat lunch. After pulling to shore and securing the boat's bow line to a tree, I pick up my baitcasting outfit, and, just for the hell of it, flip a "fat" balsa diving lure to the middle of the cove. After I retrieve about ten feet, I feel a jolt, and the rod bends. I land a bass that weighs about five pounds, our only catch after a morning of fishing.

As we munch our pork and beans and canned peaches and sip coffee, some metamorphosis occurs that arouses the bass. Who can say what causes this to happen? Can it be the time of day, or a change in the pull of the moon (see Appendix E), or a slight shift in temperature or a variation in the atmospheric pressure? It is a mystery as old as fishing, a mystery that helps make fishing so fascinating.

Anyway, on this splendid fall day, the fish change their mood at approximately 12:45 P.M., which is when Bill and I finish dining and once more begin fishing. Even though I caught the only bass so far on a baitcasting rod, I decide to try the fly rod for a few more minutes because the fly rod is what I most enjoy using. My first cast is to a cluster of submerged stumps that I can see through the clear water. The riffles the bug makes as it settles on the still water have not even dissipated when a bigger disturbance engulfs the bug. I land a bass that weighs about two pounds.

For the rest of the afternoon, I catch bass after bass on the popping bug. Bill catches some bass on his spinning rod, though not as many as I do on the fly rod and popping bug. His bass are larger than mine, however, which is often true of fish caught on spinning and baitcasting tackle versus fly tackle.

It is another fine fall day on Kerr Lake and my friend Leger Meyland and I are fishing with a guide. Leger is fishing with spinning tackle and I, of course, am using a fly rod.

Photo by Leger Meyland

Author brings in small largemouth bass on Kerr Lake.

"Cast as close as you can to those rocks," the guide says, indicating a spot in shallow water. "The wind has been blowing into these pockets for three straight days, and that should make them good spots."

Using a nine-foot fly rod, I follow the guide's instructions.

It is only about my sixth cast of the morning.

The chartreuse and yellow cork-and-feather fly lights softly on the water and I twitch the rod gently to make the fly imitate how I imagine a real insect would act. The lure vanishes in a swirl.

"There we go, right on cue," the guide says as I fight a medium-size largemouth bass to the boat.

I hold the bass up in the morning light for all to admire before I release it.

"That's a right nice one," says Leger, a Greensboro *News & Record* photographer.

"I can't believe that I caught a fish so soon," I say to the guide. "This is more than I thought I would catch on a fly rod all day. As you know, a lake like this is not the best place in the world to use a fly rod."

"Well you have to realize you are with the best guide on this lake," the guide says, evoking loud laughter from Leger and me. "I have to prove myself every day out here. If you are a woman in this business, you've got to be the best."

Our guide is Joan Holmes, the only female fishing guide on Kerr Lake. She also fishes nearby Lake Gaston and is the only female guide on that lake.

Bill Yates of Madison and I are fishing Lake Townsend, A Greensboro city water-supply lake, on a warm day in late spring. Bill is using spinning and casting rigs and I, my eight-and-a-half-foot fly rod.

Photo by Leger Meyland

Joan Holmes, a fishing guide, admires a largemouth bass caught by author on homemade popping bug at Kerr Lake.

I flip my homemade bass popping bug to the edge of some rip-rap, let it sit for a minute, then jiggle it. Something nips at the bug, and the bug sinks from sight. A small bream, I think, as I set the hook, not too hopeful that such a little fish can swallow the big bass bug.

But instead of a bream, I feel something solid and a bass—it can't weigh more than three pounds—leaps from the water. It jumps again, and again, and again.

"I've never seen a largemouth jump that much," I tell Bill as the bass clears the water still again.

(I am sure it isn't a smallmouth, a fish known for its aerial displays, because there are no smallmouth bass in the lake.)

Several times, I work the fish close to the boat only to have it vault from the water and race off again.

At last, Bill gets the landing net under the fish and dips it up. Despite its prolonged fight, the bass, a largemouth, is still very much alive, and we carefully release it. It deserves to live.

"I've never had a largemouth jump like that," I tell Bill once more. "I've never even seen a smallmouth jump that many times."

Bill, a fishing columnist and radio fishing program host, agrees.

A couple of days later, he telephones me.

"You know what I did?" he says. "I had so much fun watching you fight that bass that I got out my fly rod, which I hadn't used for years, and went down to a pond close to my house and used the rod. I caught only a few bream though."

A beautiful Sunday dawn is just breaking as my son, John, and I fish a cove beside the home of my sister and brother-in-law, Mary Sue and Marvin Rainey, on Lake Wylie, a reservoir that sits on the North Carolina–South Carolina state line near Charlotte. It is early May and the world is peaceful and calm, and the woods bordering the cove are alive with the chirping of birds.

John and I both fish with eight-and-a-half-foot fly rods and popping bugs. I have rarely seen bass hit popping bugs like this—not even on Currituck Sound during its best days, not even on other waters of Eastern North Carolina. I quickly catch my limit of bass and John loses about as many as I catch. He is still a little boy and this is one of the first times he has used a fly rod. Although he already can cast as adroitly as I can, he has difficulty keeping a tight line so he can set the hook when a bass hits, something he will soon learn to do.

It is one of the most delightful hours of fishing I have ever experienced. Soon though, a big power boat pulls into the cove. Spotting us, the driver guns his motor and thunders out of the cove. His wake churns the flooded willows and heaves big noisy waves against the shore. The bass quit hitting.

It is another soft spring day on Lake Wylie, and I am fishing with my father. Although Dad is a fine fisherman with casting and spinning equipment, he has never learned to use a fly rod. Today, he is fishing with a spinning rod.

"The fish are in shallow water," he says as he casts a Hot Spot lure toward the bank.

I, as you should guess, use my fly rod as I almost always do when I think there is even a slight chance it will catch fish. Dad quickly lands a bass. Then a small one boils up and inhales my popping bug. For about an hour, it is like that. Dad and I stay almost even in the number of fish that we each catch, though mine are generally smaller than his. Then I realize he has not caught a fish for a while.

When I turn to look, I see the reason. He has stopped fishing and is watching me. I am deeply honored. I have stopped fishing many times to watch, hypnotized, the work of fly fishermen such as Bill Black, Roger Soles, Claibourne Darden, Bill Wilkerson, John Baskervill, Don Howell and others.

I know I will never be as good a fly fisherman as any of those anglers. But I will always remember fishing this day with Dad—and not just because of that one incident. It is to be one of the last fishing trips I will make with him.

These experiences were not flukes. True, the fly rod is generally not as potent on inland lakes for catching large-mouth bass as it is on Eastern North Carolina waters. Nevertheless, it can sometimes be very deadly on both Piedmont and mountain lakes. Spinning and baitcasting rods are more effective most of the time, however, and especially when bass are feeding far below the surface of the water.

It is more difficult to fish real deep with a fly rod. A few North Carolina fly fishermen use lines that sink deep and fast. I have owned a couple of these lines but did not enjoy using them. To me, a fast sinking line, especially one that sinks throughout its length, is too unwieldy. After a cast, you have to strain to get a deep sinking line to the top of the water so that you can lift it out to make another cast. It is also hard on your fly rod, I think. A sink tip line, one whose first few feet sink, is easier to use. But I don't even like that type line.

John Baskervill agrees.

"I once used sinking lines," he says. "I even made sinking lines."

He used sections of lead-core trolling line, splicing them to the ends of regular fly line.

"But now," John says. "I just don't see the need for a sinking line."

When John wants to fish deep with a fly that doesn't sink deep naturally, he uses split shot on his leader. I don't even do that very often. It took me a long time to learn to use that kind of heavy rig without hitting myself in the back of the head every few casts, and I still occasionally hit my head when I use split shots on my leader. And that smarts.

"It's not all that hard to use," John says, referring to a leader weighted with split shot. "You just have to adjust your timing."

John uses the fly rod more than any other type of tackle, no matter where he is: on inland lakes or on Eastern North Carolina fresh and brackish waters and no matter whether it is spring, summer, fall or winter. He occasionally will put down his fly rod and fish spinning and baitcasting equipment. But that's relatively rare, considering that he fishes just about every day.

You fish a bass fly rod in inland North Carolina lakes about the same way you would fish other types of tackle: on top of the water in the spring and fall and sometimes even in summer early in the morning and late in the afternoon. In the summer and winter you fish under water, except that—as mentioned earlier—most North Carolina fly rod anglers don't fish as deep as anglers using other gear sometimes do. That's not always true, of course. A few fly rod anglers do sometimes fish deep. But most don't. In fact, most bass that are caught on a fly rod are caught relatively close to the surface. Blewett Falls Lake in Richmond and Anson Counties is one of the best of North Carolina's inland lakes on which to fly fish for largemouth. It is more shallow than most inland lakes and has a lot of cover, making it an especially good place to use popping bugs. Generally speaking, fall is the best time to fish Blewett Falls. The water is usually clearer then than during the spring.

In some North Carolina lakes, largemouth bass sporadically school on or near the surface in both deep and shallow water. When they do that, you can catch them on about any floating cork or deer hair bug or underwater streamer or about anything else you care to throw at them.

Lake Tillery is the best lake I have ever fished for schooling largemouth bass. The bass usually congregate on top in late summer and on into fall. I was fishing Tillery with Bill Black the first time I ever saw largemouth bass do that in large numbers.

We had gone to Tillery in the early fall to fish for schooling white bass. When we saw fish slashing the surface, we thought they were white bass. But they were largemouth, and they schooled throughout the day. We caught some largemouth, and Bill caught a striped bass.

I have since witnessed the phenomenon of schooling largemouth bass many times. Once while Doris Dale and I were fishing with Mary Jane and John Peterson, Doris Dale and I (fishing in our boat while John and Mary Jane fished in theirs) saw fish making a commotion on the surface of the water several times during the day. Again, I thought they were white bass, because I had fished there a few weeks earlier when white bass (see Chapter Thirteen) were schooling all over the lake. But this time, the schooling fish were largemouth bass.

When largemouth school on the surface on Tillery, they tear into schools of minnows, sending showers of the frightened little fish a foot into the air. For a long time, however, Tillery was the only lake that I regularly fished without being able to catch a bass on a fly rod. I tried many times before abandoning my beloved fly rod in favor of spinning or casting rods.

I give Bill Wilkerson credit for inspiring me to give the fly rod another chance on Tillery.

We went to Lake Tillery at my suggestion.

"I can't wait for you to see the white bass schooling," I told Bill, who is a good enough caster with the fly rod to be certified as an instructor. "I know they will hit a streamer or a popper. They'll hit anything when they are schooling on top as they almost always do this time of the year."

Of course, you know what happened.

We made two trips to Tillery without seeing a single school of white bass.

But the largemouth were schooling sporadically.

Bill caught several. Although schooling bass are usually small, one that Bill hooked put up such a struggle, I thought for a while it was a striped bass. At first, it didn't jump as largemouth usually do when they are hooked near the top of the water. Instead, it made several splendid runs. Bill was using a light, seven-and-a-half-foot trout fly rod, which made the fight even more exciting to watch. Bill's fly was a Marabou Leech that he had tied himself.

The bass was not a big one but it made up for its size with its fight. Bill rewarded the bass's spunk by carefully releasing it. I was so impressed with the battle that Bill's fish put up that I again began using a fly rod when I fished Lake Tillery and have since caught, while using a fly rod, some nice bass.

I have also seen largemouth school in other places including in the shallow waters of Eastern North Carolina. The fly rod is perfect to use when this happens because they do not seem to be as spooky as are inland schooling bass. I remember when my son, Conrad, and I fished Scranton Creek east of Belhaven one early November day when bass were feeding on top. I caught fish on my bass bug about every cast while Conrad picked up an occasional one on his Tiny Torpedo.

But I have never seen largemouth schooling anywhere else the way they school on Tillery. They are easy to catch then, if you can get close enough to get your bug or streamer to them.

Largemouth and smallmouth bass, along with white bass, also school on North Carolina's deep mountain lakes, especially Fontana. But there they usually school in late spring or early summer.

Also mountain lake bass, even when they are not schooling, often come to the top to feed during late spring and early summer. They do this so enthusiastically there that some mountain anglers have devised a method of fishing that is similar to fishing for bonefish in the Florida Keys. In the mountains, though, it is called "jump fishing."

Jump fishing for bass and bonefishing have several things in common: Each is a combination of stalking and hunting and fishing. In bonefishing in the subtropics, you fish the flats, which are long stretches of extremely shallow water, all about the same depth. In jump fishing in North Carolina mountain lakes, you usually fish deep water.

In both the subtropics and North Carolina mountains, however, you stand in the boat with your fly line coiled at your feet or the bail of your spinning reel cocked so you can cast the instant you see a sign of a fish. In bonefishing, the sign can be a mud puff or a tail or fin protruding from the water; in the mountains, the fish give themselves away by swirling on the surface.

The reason you have to cast quickly in bonefishing is that the fish are skittish, and the slightest noise will send them racing away. In jump fishing on the mountain lakes, you have to cast without delay because the fish don't like the warm water on top and immediately dive back down to the coolness of the depths.

"But if you're ready to throw right when he jumps, and you're within striking distance of him, you'll pretty well get a strike every time," said Luther Turpin, an expert at fishing on mountain lakes.

In jump fishing on North Carolina mountain lakes, most spin fishermen use Tiny Torpedoes or similar topwater lures. Fly rod fishermen use popping bugs or other floating lures. But streamers can also be effective on mountain lakes. When you use streamers, especially weighted ones like the Clouser Minnows, you stand a chance of not only getting the bass that are schooling on top but also those that are just under the surface and have not had time to dive back to deep water.

Jump fishing can yield white bass and smallmouth bass in addition to largemouth bass.

Photo by Bill Black

Curtis Laughlin and big smallmouth bass he caught on New River.

Chapter Five

Whitewater Smallmouth: Refreshing Fishing

Wading and fishing for smallmouth bass on a North Carolina whitewater river is pleasant even when the fishing is not good. The river tumbling downstream, gurgling over boulders, and splashing against the bank creates images that are pleasing to the eye and a symphony that is pleasing to the ear.

It is especially enjoyable on summer days when the heat in the North Carolina lowlands is so brutal that it saps your energy and softens the asphalt on parking lots and city streets. Then, wading a mountain river is like entering a different world. You stand in the river, shaded by tall hardwood and evergreen trees while clear, cool water washes around your waders or bare legs. You feel comfortable and at peace.

There are other reasons for fishing this kind of water with a fly rod, even when you don't catch a bass—which isn't very often. It is usually solitary and pastoral. On some days, an occasional canoe, jonboat or rubber raft will drift by you. But the water is too shallow to accommodate any craft that produces more noise than those.

I make a smallmouth bass fishing trip from time to time with my friends, Bill Black and John Baskervill. They always catch more fish than I do. But I enjoy the trips. Even when I only catch rock bass, also known as "redeye"—a scrappy fish that hits the same flies or popping bugs that a smallmouth bass hits but which does not have the stamina of a smallmouth.

I remember one of the first trips I made with John and Bill. John had lived in the mountains for several years and first fished the New River on July 4, 1948, when he caught a smallmouth that weighed four and a quarter pounds—a big smallmouth indeed. That turned him into a smallmouth addict, and he has fished the river so many times since then that he can read its water almost as adeptly as you and I read the morning newspaper.

He now usually fishes mountain rivers with his fly rod, which in recent years has usually been a moderate-priced eight-and-a-half footer, and has caught and released innumerable smallmouth.

He also has come to admire the friendliness and intelligence of mountain folk and has made many friends along the New River. After he visits with them a few minutes they say, sure, you're welcome to park your car in our yards while you fish.

John also respects the self-reliance of the people who live along the river. To illustrate the hardiness of those folk, he tells a story that may be a joke but could be true.

"Some of these areas are very remote," he said as we traveled down a winding mountain dirt road on my first small-mouth trip in years. "Remember the blizzard that hit the area in the late 1950s or early 1960s?"

After the storm, according to John, relief workers fought through high snow drifts to a secluded home and banged on the door. A woman, wiping her hands on her apron, answered the knock.

"We're from the Red Cross," the would-be rescuer announced.

"We already gave," the woman said matter-of-factly.

John is one of the state's best all-around fly rod fishermen. Bill is good, too. On this trip to the New River, we all used fly rods. John and I used eight-and-a-half-foot rods. Bill used a nine-foot rod. All our rods were matched for Number Eight lines.

Soon after we struggled into our chest waders and slid into the cool rushing waters of the South Fork of the New River, John hooked and landed and released a smallmouth bass. But nobody else caught anything at that spot. We drove to West Jefferson where, over hamburgers, Bill and John decided to try the New River's North Fork.

We drove to the North Fork and again donned our waders and eased into the water. There John and Bill each caught and released about a dozen smallmouth and a number of "redeye." Then we returned to the South Fork, fishing a different stretch than the one we had fished in the morning, and John caught several smallmouth. Bill caught more redeye.

Most of the smallmouth and redeye hit medium-sized cork poppers, though Bill caught several redeye on a spinner fly, which is a combination of a small or medium-sized spinner trailed by a bushy fly. John caught some smallmouth on a Clouser Minnow, a fast sinking streamer fly.

I caught only a little smallmouth and a redeye. Excuse? My waders leaked and filled with water. With the water sloshing around in the waders, and the river surging around me, I fought just to keep my footing on the slick submerged rocks.

Where we were, wading is the most practical way to fish. But footing is often treacherous, and felt glued to the bottom of the feet of your waders helps you maintain your equilibrium. Or if you are wading "wet," in pants or shorts, carpet glued to the soles of your tennis shoes will give you traction. You also can buy felt soles (see Appendix B) to glue to your shoes or to replace the felt on your waders. A wading staff is helpful (see Chapter One).

The trip Bill, John and I made that fall would have been enjoyable even if we had not caught any fish. We saw just four other anglers, and the murmur of the translucent river was soothing to the soul. Colorful wildflowers studded the bank and filled the air with perfume. It rained for a while in the late afternoon, leaving an agreeable nip in the air and the mountains wreathed in mist.

On every fishing trip I make to the New River, I see things that will remain in my memory for a long time.

On another trip I made with Bill and John, Bill parked the car beside the river, and we slithered down the bank to the water. Soon after we settled in, an underwater shadow glided by me.

I first thought it was a big carp. But when I looked again, I saw that it was a large animal with a big flat tail. A beaver. It did not seem to be even a little afraid of me. It came so close I could have touched it with my fly rod. I shouted for Bill, who was fishing nearby, but he could not see it from where he was. I hoped it would get out of the water so Bill could observe it. But it disappeared, apparently swimming under the bank.

After lunch on that same day, we went by Larry Stanbery's sawmill near Boone. Larry took us to one of his favorite places on the river to fish.

"Look," Larry said, pointing to some tracks as we eased down the bank of the river. "Look at where a big deer has been."

You can learn a lot by fishing for smallmouth in a North Carolina mountain river with anglers such as Bill Black and John Baskervill.

I noticed, for example, that Bill and John usually wade a reasonable distance from the bank they want to fish and move downstream instead of up as trout fishermen usually do.

North Carolina smallmouth rivers are usually wider than the typical North Carolina trout stream, Bill points out. Consequently, mud and silt that you stir up by wading downstream does not disturb the fish as long as you stay away from the bank to which you are casting and make moderately long casts.

John mentioned another reason for wading downstream.

"You'll soon get tired from fighting the current if you wade upstream," he said.

When fishing the banks of smallmouth streams, both John and Bill aim their casts so that their flies or bugs land as near as possible to spots about two inches from the bank.

They also fish riffles. Bill prefers to cast to a riffle from the side, hitting the beginning of the riffle, and then letting the current wash his bug or streamer down the choppy water and to the pool below. If he can't approach the riffle from the side, he will cast down to it but still let the current wash his fly downstream to the calm water. When he uses streamers, he likes something that is weighted so that it will hug the bottom on its journey through the fast water.

John has a different philosophy about riffles.

"I just cast to every spot where I think there may be a fish," he says.

Bill and John occasionally catch nice mountain trout while fishing for smallmouth in Western North Carolina.

Most of the trout they catch are brown trout and, for the most part, the trout hit underwater offerings. But Bill once caught a big rainbow on, of all things, a cork bass bug.

The trout was lurking near a bush that was covered with Japanese Beetles. It obviously was eating the beetles that fell in the water because when Bill cleaned the fish it had eleven beetles in its stomach. Bill and John release most of the bass they catch on the New River—and elsewhere for that matter.

Most trout, of course, are farther upstream from the places where you catch smallmouth.

Vince Davis of Lewisville was fishing the New River and using a Woolly Bugger when he caught a smallmouth that weighed seven-and-a-half pounds on calibrated scales. Perhaps larger smallmouths have been caught on fly rods in North Carolina. I just have never heard of them.

Before leaving home for a smallmouth bass fishing trip, it is a good idea to call ahead to inquire about the condition of the stream you plan to fish. A rain will often muddy the rivers, but the water can clear quickly. When the water is red, Bill Black and John Baskervill wait another day before making the drive to the mountains.

John is in the lumber business and has many mountain friends with whom he can check before planning a small-mouth fishing trip. He has another good source he can call. His son, Robert, lives in Boone and keeps John informed about fishing conditions.

84

Photo by Vince Davis

Huge smallmouth caught on New River by Vince Davis using rod he built.

But even when you check the night before you leave home and learn that the river is clear then, it can become muddy by the time you arrive the next morning. If that does happen, however, you don't have to abandon your plans. You can often salvage the trip by fishing for trout (see Chapter Eight) in smaller streams at higher elevations. Even when rivers are red with mud, trout streams are often clear.

The New River is not the only good smallmouth bass stream in North Carolina. The Watauga River around Boone is another. You fish it with a fly rod about the same way that Bill Black and John Baskervill fish the New River.

Other places in Western North Carolina where you can catch smallmouth on a fly rod with varying degrees of success include some parts (usually the lower reaches) of these streams: Cane River, Cheoah River, Elk Creek, French Broad River, Linville River, Little Tennessee River, Mitchell River, Nolichucky River, Roaring River, South and North Toe Rivers, and Wilson Creek.

The Uwharrie River in the Uwharrie Mountains also holds smallmouth bass. For years, the smallmouth fishing in that river has been known to only a relatively few anglers. Even now, John Baskervill would just as soon it remained a secret.

"I don't even like to talk about it," he says.

But as a favor, he will reluctantly discuss it in general terms.

"Somebody studied it back in the early 1960s and decided that it would support smallmouth," he says.

As a result, smallmouth were stocked in the Uwharrie. Some thrived.

"Barnes and Cedar Creeks, tributaries to the Uwharrie, are especially good," John says.

86

Those two creeks are in Montgomery County. The creeks, where they are shallow, may be fished by wading.

Some of the smallmouth have spilled out into Lake Tillery, especially around the mouth of the Uwharrie River. The lake and the lower and deeper reaches of the river should be fished from a boat.

When you do wade, no matter which stream you fish, it is a good idea to fish with a buddy. Also, use caution even when fishing with somebody else. Although long stretches of North Carolina smallmouth rivers are shallow, some spots are very deep. Every so often, anglers get swept away by the current and are drowned or beaten to death against boulders.

Photo by Buck Paysour

Marshall Coble, smallmouth fishing guide, and the canoe he uses.

Chapter Six

Other Smallmouth Fishing

Wading a North Carolina mountain stream for smallmouth bass is fun, all right. So is canoeing it with a friend such as Marshall Coble of Greensboro.

Marshall spends many of his spring, summer and fall weekends and holidays guiding smallmouth bass anglers on the James River in Virginia and, occasionally, on the New River in Virginia and the New River in North Carolina. But he does not guide professionally every weekend. He reserves several of his weekends and holidays for a busman's—more correctly, an angler's—holiday. He uses those weekends to fish with his buddies just for fun.

During the week, he is a draftsman and when he is not fishing or working at his principal job, he is a member of All Star Rods' field staff. He also helps promote the fine custom-made rods crafted by his friend, Bill Poe of Staley.

Marshall remembers how he came to love the smallmouth bass. Interestingly, it was not on the kind of water that he now prefers to fish. He caught his first smallmouth on Smith Mountain Lake in Virginia.

"It was such an acrobatic fish and was so strong," he says. "It jumped I don't know how many times. Catching it ruined me."

That happened in the mid-1970s.

Several years after landing that first smallmouth, Marshall discovered river smallmouth bass fishing and fell in love with it. He spent much time studying the habits of the fish and also became an expert canoeist.

He has had some unusual experiences while fishing whitewater rivers. On several occasions, muskellunge have attacked and shredded smallmouth that Marshall or his clients hooked.

Nothing that unusual happened the day I fished the New River with Marshall. But it was still one of the most fascinating and enjoyable days I have ever spent on the water.

Marshall picked me up at home before daylight on a nippy, early fall day. His canoe was lashed to the top of his four-wheel-drive Dodge Ram. We stopped in North Wilkesboro and ate a fine country breakfast. Then we drove on to West Jefferson where we met Marshall's friends, Mike Poe (no relation to rod maker Bill Poe) and Keith Hartzog, at Keith's home. They had already loaded their canoe in the back of Keith's four-wheel-drive Ford pickup.

From there, we traveled down winding mountain roads to the New River. After unloading both canoes, Marshall and Keith drove their vehicles downstream and left Keith's at a bridge where we would be taking the canoes out of the water at the end of the day. That would save us from having to paddle back up the river, almost an impossible task.

While Keith and Marshall were gone, Mike waded out to a rock and, as early morning mist swirled around him, caught several smallmouth on his spinning outfit.

After Keith and Marshall returned in Marshall's four-wheel-drive vehicle, we launched both canoes. I fished with Marshall and immediately got two strikes. But the fish hit the popping bug short, and I did not hook them.

Alas, I only caught rock ("redeye") bass that day on my fly rod. But they were fun to catch. Marshall caught a number of smallmouth and redeye on both spinning and fly casting gear even though he fished only sporadically, devoting most of his time to handling the canoe and positioning it for me to cast.

Marshall usually fishes the James in Virginia where he and the anglers he guides sometimes catch and release as many as two hundred smallmouth a day. Marshall has also has some sensational days on the New in North Carolina, but it is more fickle than the James.

We had come to the New on this day at my suggestion. I like the river because it is one of the country's most beautiful, even prettier than the James.

Marshall and I drifted, sometimes tumbled, down the boulder-strewn whitewater. We passed green meadows, picturesque farms, long stretches of virgin forest. Mountains, clothed in blue haze, often loomed above us.

Deep, calm pools over which we floated were so diaphanous I had the feeling of being levitated on nothing but air.

All day, a gangly blue heron preceded our canoe. He seemed curious about us, though not at all afraid. He would sit on a sand bar, perch on a tree that had fallen in the water, or stand motionless in shallow water with one of his long legs crooked under his body and peer at us. Standing in the water, he looked like a dignified one-legged old man who had decided to go wading.

When we drew near, the heron would lumber clumsily into the air. But once airborne, he flew with a swan-like grace to a new spot to once again await our approach.

Sometimes we did not see him for five minutes or so and I would say, "I believe our friend has left us."

But then we would round a bend and Marshall would point and say, "There he is."

The heron was just one of the enchanting things we saw during the day. An occasional kingfisher darted from side to side of the river, chattering at our intrusion. Several rafts of mallards shared the water with us.

After we ran one reach of fast water, we heard a rustling in the undergrowth at the edge of the river on our left side. Then, a mother deer and her two fawns came into sight and stepped into the river, apparently with intentions of crossing. After staring at us for a long moment, they turned, kicked up a shower of rainbow-tinged spray and bounded back into the forest.

The day was bright and the touch of frost that had greeted our arrival in the morning soon disappeared as the air warmed. At noon, we pulled our canoes up to a boulder as big as a tobacco barn in the middle of the river, got out, climbed up and sat on the warm stone, and enjoyed the panorama below while we ate.

Marshall caught his smallmouth on fly rods made, of course, by Bill Poe and All Star. Most of the fish hit a small Clouser Minnow that he tied himself. He also likes popping bugs, Woolly Buggers and Woolly Worms, and similar flies for river fishing. He furnishes equipment for anglers who do not have their own. I caught my redeye bass on a Zonker and a home-made popper.

Late in the afternoon, we passed a farm where some men and women were harvesting tobacco while listening to a football game on a truck radio. We yelled to ask them who was winning. The University of North Carolina, my alma mater, was ahead. But that seemed far away and unimportant.

Sometimes, Marshall and his anglers get out of the canoe and wade at various spots on the river. For that reason, he had suggested that I bring along an extra set of clothes and spare shoes, which he tucked, along with my camera, into a waterproof bag. The dry clothes would also come in handy if we waded or in the unlikely event that we should turn over, he said.

Marshall is an expert canoeist and he guided us through long stretches of swift water without even coming close to tipping. He stationed the canoe so perfectly for casting to likely spots that I didn't need to get out and wade.

I did change my socks and shoes at the end of the trip. The ones I had worn all day were slightly moist from the water that had dripped into the canoe's floor from Marshall's paddle. But other than that little dampness, I was dry.

The sun was waning when we arrived at our take-out spot at the bridge where Keith's truck was parked. We loaded both canoes on the truck and returned to where Marshall's four-wheel-drive was waiting, then transferred Marshall's canoe to his vehicle.

When Marshall dropped me at my home that night, he promised to take me fishing again. I resolved to hold him to that. And he did. But this time he took me to the James River in Virginia. There I caught more than sixty smallmouth, most of them on a fly rod, while fishing with Marshall and two of his buddies, Virginians Ricky Moore and Doug McHaney. Marshall said even that was not an exceptional day. I believed him.

The canoe in which Marshall and I fished both the James New Rivers was surprisingly comfortable. But maybe you would rather fly fish for smallmouth bass on more placid waters and in something a little more roomy. There is a way. North Carolina mountain lakes have smallmouth bass.

True, catching lake smallmouth on fly tackle in mountain lakes will be more challenging because the water is much deeper. But you can do it, and it's fun.

While fishing deep mountain lakes, you can sometimes even catch smallmouth on topwater bass bugs. I remember one mid-June trip to Fontana Lake with my son, Conrad. We asked around at tackle stores and service stations about what lures we should use and how we should fish for bass—both largemouth and smallmouth.

Everybody gave the same answer in almost the same words: "Fish deep."

That's what we did for most of the morning. We used every deep-running baitcasting and spinning lure in our tackle boxes. It was no use.

I became bored.

Then I remembered a saying that James A. King, a fine fly rod fishermen, had coined to explain why he liked to fish a popping bug or other topwater fly.

"If I'm going to pay the price of admission," he said, "I want to see the picture show."

So I put down my casting rod and picked up my nine-foot fly rod, tied a deer hair bug on the end of the leader, and cast to some flooded willows. I let the bug rest for a second, then twitched it several times, then retrieved it about six feet hard, creating bubbles in its wake. Nothing happened. I lifted the bug off the water and shot it to another spot in the willows.

It had barely settled on the water when the bug faded from sight in a commotion. I didn't even have to set the hook. A nice fish cleared the water, then made jump after jump, letting me know it was a smallmouth.

After that, I caught a number of other smallmouth on my bug, and Conrad caught several more on his spinning rod and a Tiny Torpedo.

But most anglers who fish mountain lakes with fly rods say that you'll usually stand a better chance of catching smallmouth bass on a sinking fly than on a floating one. They mention the same flies that anglers use on other waters for both smallmouth and largemouth bass. These, of course, include Clouser Minnows, Deceivers, Woolly Buggers, Woolly Worms, spinner flies, Zonkers and similar things. Smallmouth prefer flies that are larger than those generally used for trout and panfish but smaller than those usually used for largemouth. Some anglers even use sinking lines on the lakes, but that is far from a universal method.

Smallmouth can be caught in just about every North Carolina mountain lake. Lake James, on the Catawba River chain, is about the lowest down the mountains that you can expect to readily catch them. Most of the smallmouth lakes, including James, also have (see Chapters Four and Thirteen) largemouth and white bass and some even have trout—which makes fishing them even more interesting.

Don Howell with record brown trout.

Chapter Seven

Mountain Trout: Classic Fly Rod Fish

When most fishermen think of fly fishing, especially North Carolina fly fishing, mountain trout is the fish that first comes to mind. It is the classic fly rod fish.

And when I think of classic North Carolina mountain trout fly fishermen, Don Howell of Brevard in Transylvania County is one of the first that comes to mind. For years, I dreamed of fishing with Don. But on the morning that I finally got that opportunity, I wondered if I had chosen the wrong time.

When he and I arrived at the Davidson River near Brevard and looked at the water, a knot formed in the pit of my stomach. You know the feeling. It's the same as the one some sports fishermen get when they arrive at their favorite fishing lake to find the water roiling muddy and over the banks. Or hundreds of boat trailers parked at the ramp indicating a bass club is holding a huge tournament.

But the water on the Davidson River that mid-July day when Don Howell and I fished for mountain trout was not crowded or muddy. It was, in fact, the opposite of muddy. It was as clear as a dry martini and low—sorry conditions for trout fishing.

Even Don, a legendary fly tyer and custom rod maker and trout fisherman, was pessimistic about fishing prospects.

"But when conditions are anywhere near good, the Davidson River is the best place in the state to catch big brown trout," he said as if apologizing in advance for what he expected was going to be unproductive fishing.

Don, however, was to soon prove that he could catch trout even in low and crystalline water.

It was abnormally hot that summer and the weather forecast for the day we fished called for temperatures to soar into the nineties, setting records, even in the mountains of Transylvania County. For that reason, we had decided to fish only in the morning. But in those few hours, Don landed more than a dozen trout. He caught all three species common to North Carolina: brown, rainbow and even one brook.

The brook trout is a rarity for that section of the Davidson River. It is more at home in smaller and cooler streams at higher elevations than where we were fishing.

The stretch of river we fished was narrow and did not have room for two anglers to fish side by side. Don, a gentleman and a true sportsman, kept insisting that I fish in front of him. I finally relented.

My back casts frequently snagged on the low-hanging limbs that protruded over the water. I have great pride in my ability to drive a bass bug or a bass or saltwater streamer even into the teeth of a gale and cast it close to where I want it to go—and often catch fish. But fishing again in a narrow, tree- and bush-lined trout stream made me decide that my trout fly casting needed improving. I also decided that my friend Rich Preyer, a former congressman and an avid trout fisherman, might be right when he said that catching trout on a fly rod is more difficult than catching bass on a fly rod.

Don Howell and I later discussed that very question. We agreed that, like beauty, the answer as to which is the most difficult is in the eye of the beholder. It is like trying to decide whether blondes, brunettes or redheads make the best-looking women.

Anyway, on that summer day on the Davidson River, I made one decision after I snagged on bushes several times. I concluded that it was more fun to watch Don fish than to fish myself. After all, I had come to learn from him. I could fish later. And I was not disappointed by what I saw.

A fly rod in Don's hands became a thing of grace. He used a rod he had built himself, an eight footer, matched for a Number Five line. Because the water was so clear and shallow, he had to make casts longer than those often needed for North Carolina trout fishing. Sometimes in really tight quarters, he made roll casts. At other places, he made casts that called for lengthy back casts. Either way, his fly landed softly wherever he wanted it to go. He usually cast sidearm and never once snagged on bushes on his front casts. Even on his back casts, he hung up only a few times.

Don varies the length of his leader depending on the condition of the water. On this day, he used a nine-and-a-half-foot leader, longer than he normally would have used, because the water was so low and so clear that the fly line could more easily spook the trout.

"It's a good rule of thumb under most conditions to use a leader that is about the length of your rod," he said later.

His leader's tippet was four-pound test.

"I use that size leader more than any other," he explained. "I seldom go below two-pound test."

He prefers knotted leaders because he thinks they roll over better.

"But if you use knotted leaders, you need to check your knots from time-to-time because that is where the weakness is," he warned.

He ties a twelve-inch section of stiff sixty-pound-test leader material between his line and leader to help turn his fly over.

He wears wading shoes with felt bottoms and wades "wet," or without hip boots or chest waders, during warm weather.

On this day, Don fished a G. Neil fly (see Chapter Two) that he ties. It is a popular nymph for both trout and bream fishing.

"It is especially good when the water is low and clear, like it is now," Don explained.

When he fishes the G. Neil or any other nymph, he almost always uses the eight-foot rod he was casting on this sweltering summer day.

"It's a good rod for nymph fishing," he explained. "In fact, I probably use that rod more than any other no matter what kind of trout fishing I'm doing."

For North Carolina fishing, he rarely uses a sinking line even for nymph fishing.

"You can detect a strike easier with a floating line," he says. "You can tell when your line does anything unusual. That's difficult to see if your line is under the water."

Don seldom uses strike indicators (see Chapter Two) but thinks they could help a beginning trout fisherman who has difficulty telling when something has picked up his nymph.

Later, I stopped by Don's home to ask him what other advice he would give someone who was just learning to fish a fly rod for trout.

"The most important thing is presentation," he answered. "You have to be an extremely good caster. That's doesn't mean coming close....A lot of fish I catch are ones I've seen. If you see a trout and your fly doesn't go just about exactly where it is supposed to go, chances are the trout is not going to take it.

"If you throw your fly behind him and off to one side, he'll often turn and take your fly without looking close at it. If you put it anywhere else, he will come look at it, and maybe also at your leader, and then usually turn and go away. Also, your fly has to land softly on the water."

Any other advice?

"I can't over-emphasize how important it is to wade quietly," Don said. "I've fished with people who, when they waded, sounded like they were Evinrude outboard motors going up the stream. You can't catch any fish doing that.

"If you make a lot of commotion, it's as if your house and table started shaking while you were sitting there eating a T-bone steak. You're going to get frightened and stop eating. It's the same way with trout. If one is feeding and a fisherman is not a cautious wader and runs waves to that trout, the trout is not going to take that fisherman's fly.

"You know how it is when you're in swimming and you duck under the water and how loud it sounds when somebody claps two rocks together under the water? That's about the same thing a trout hears if you stumble over rocks while you're wading."

Don, of course, wades upstream so that any silt stirred up can not disturb the fish in front of him. Many fly rod anglers who fish for smallmouth bass usually do the opposite because of the differences in the streams (see Chapter Five) they generally fish.

Anything else a novice trout angler needs to know?

"Yes," Don said. "My dad was a real stickler about dress. And he was right. If I met him on a trout stream, and I was dressed the wrong way, he'd send me back home to change clothes. For North Carolina trout fishing, he thought you should dress in dark clothes that blended in with the foliage. Anything dull. Not white or red. I've seen people out West wearing bright clothes, vests that reflected the sunlight. I don't think that makes that much of a difference out there where there is no foliage. But it makes a big difference around here."

About the only times of the year when Don doesn't fish is in the dead of winter and, even then, he has been known to try his luck on days when he could wade without freezing to death.

What is his favorite month to fish for trout?

"October. That's when I catch the most trout during typical years. But I catch more real big fish during most years in July than during any other month. I know this sounds crazy, but I catch more big trout during the full of the moon in July than during any other time."

There was no full moon the July day I fished with Don. But he did well anyway.

His rod bent on one of his first casts, and he landed the brook trout. Shortly after that, he hooked and landed a small brown trout. The trout sparkled gold in the sunlight that seeped through the overhead foliage. Don caught a couple more browns before landing his first rainbow, a fish whose dazzling colors lived up to its name.

After landing each trout, Don carefully dipped his hands in the river before removing the G. Neil nymph from the fish's mouth. He then gently released the fish. One rainbow briefly turned over on its belly after being turned loose.

"It's disoriented," Don said, reaching for the fish once more and moving it back and forth in the water to help it breathe.

Revived, the fish scooted off.

"The trout is too valuable a resource to catch one time and kill," Don declared as if he was talking about something sacred.

The water was so translucent you could see trout swimming in it thirty to forty feet in front of you. Although we waded with stealth, many trout scooted away long before we could get close enough to cast to them.

Despite what appeared to be the poor fishing conditions, Don caught one brown trout that was about sixteen inches long and one that was about eighteen inches long.

Don is a retired high school teacher who grew up fishing the South Toe River for trout in the Spruce Pine area. He was so young when he started fishing, he can't even remember the first time he went. He does recall that his father, Don Daughtery Howell, fished for trout while carrying him on his shoulders.

"I remember hearing people talk about the time Dad hooked a big trout while fishing with my older brother, Dwight, on his shoulders," Don, an intelligent and good-natured man, recalled. "Dwight got so excited that he flailed around and got his hands in front of Dad's eyes so that Dad couldn't see. Dad naturally lost that trout, but they say that he did not get upset with Dwight."

After growing up and graduating from college, Don taught school in Rutherfordton. Although he liked living and teaching in Rutherfordton, he wanted to get back to an area where the trout fishing was better. So he applied for a teaching job in Brevard and was hired.

Don and his brother, Dwight, were good fishing buddies, and also very good trout fishermen. Dwight, fishing Armstrong Creek in McDowell County in 1972, caught the state record brown trout—one that weighed seven pounds and eight ounces. Two years later, another angler broke that record with a brown trout that weighed seven pounds, twelve ounces, caught in the Davidson River. Guess who broke Dwight's record? His brother, Don. They may have been the only brothers ever to hold back-to-back North Carolina state trout records. Since then, of course, Don's record has been broken by other anglers.

Dwight and Don were partners in the fly-tying and rod-making venture. After Dwight died, Don continued building rods and tying flies by himself. The rods and flies are much in demand by anglers from all over the country. Don's son, Kevin, now helps with the fly-tying and rod-building businesses.

Don and Kevin Howell tie just about any fly that anybody wants them to tie, but their favorite nymphs for North Carolina fishing include the G. Neil, Tellico Nymph, Black Nymph, Don's Stone Fly, Yellow Hammer Nymph, Superfly, Yellow Stone Fly, and Sheep Fly.

"In this part of the country, you just need a fly that looks like a bug," says Don. "You could probably get by with four or five nymphs."

Don and Kevin tie a couple of other flies that are especially effective. One is called simply "The Bug." It is a nymph with rubber legs.

"The legs kick, giving it a little life," says Don. "I think that little extra kick might be the thing that persuades a following fish to take it."

Another superb fly that he and Kevin tie is the Hot Creek Special. It is especially productive in low and clear water. It is made largely from peacock and looks like a Japanese Beetle. Don uses floatant on his leader and fishes the Hot Creek Special as a nymph just under the surface of the water.

Two other wet flies Don likes to fish are the Woolly Bugger and the Bitch Creek.

Although Don has been fishing for trout longer than he can remember, he only started nymph fishing in the mid-1960s when he was a student at Appalachian State University.

"That's when I first read about nymph fishing," he says. "Until then, I used only dry flies."

So Don started nymph fishing. But it took a while for him to convert his father.

"Dad was a die-hard dry fly fisherman most of his life," Don recalls. "He said, 'If I'm not to catch any fish, I'd rather not catch them on dry flies than on anything else.'"

Then Don's father discovered the Sheep Fly, a wet fly created by Newland Sanders of Lenoir, and began using that fly when dry flies would not tease trout into rising. The Sheep Fly continues to be popular with Don. Using that fly, he and Dwight, in just one summer, caught thirty-two trout that measured over eighteen inches each.

"We got our first Sheep Flies from George 'Cap' Weise, a fishing friend who got them from Newland Sanders," Don says. "I've taken all kinds of fish on that fly: trout, crappie, bream, and even carp. It has wings that pulsate, and I think it looks a lot like a minnow swimming along."

(Nymph flies sink and imitate insects in their larval stage.)

When Don does use dry flies in North Carolina, he usually chooses some deer hair patterns that he originated or Royal Wulffs, Parachute Adamses, Male Adamses, or Female

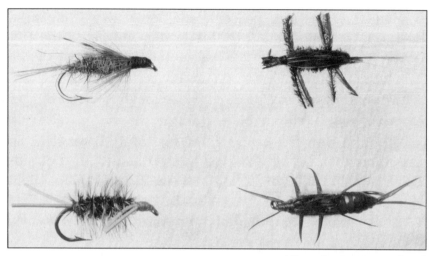

Photo by Leger Meyland

Some of the wet (sinking) flies tied by Don Howell. Top: Sheep Fly; left; Hot Creek Special, right. Bottom: The Bug, left, Superfly, right.

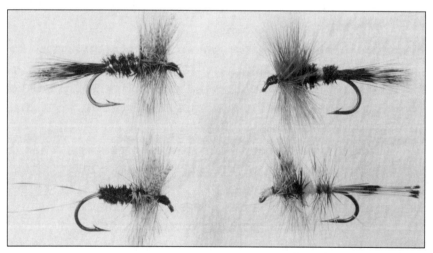

Photo by Leger Meyland

Typical dry (floating) flies made by Don Howell. Top: Don's Pet, left; Tennessee Wulff, right. Bottom: Near Nuff, left; Adams Variant, right.

Adamses. Although Don prefers Size Ten nymphs and Size Twelve dry flies for most trout fishing, he will use smaller or larger ones depending on whether the water is low, high, clear, dingy and so on.

"If water is high I will use nymphs as large as a Number Four and, on rare occasions, even a Number Two," he says.

(A fly size is designated by the size of its hook, which generally is measured in even number sizes. A Number Four fly, for example, is tied on a Number Four Hook. And the smaller the number of the hook, the larger the hook is. In other words, a Number Four is much larger than a Number Sixteen, and a Number Six is one size smaller than a Number Eight and so on.)

Don seldom fishes a fly smaller than a Sixteen and only rarely uses even a Sixteen.

"I think that's one mistake many beginning trout fishermen make," he said. "They go into sporting good stores and see all the tiny flies, and some people who own the stores say 'You need tiny flies.' But fishermen don't need them."

John Baskervill says much the same thing about fishing small flies (see Chapter Eight and Appendix C).

Bill Wilkerson agrees. He usually starts out a normal day's fishing in North Carolina with slightly smaller flies than Don Howell uses on an average day. Bill thinks a Number Twelve is a good all-around size.

"If you're not getting any interest on those size flies, I think it's wise to go to something larger or smaller," Bill says. "But only as a last resort will I try an Eighteen or smaller. On a rare occasion I might try something like a little Midge."

A midge is tiny, not much larger than a gnat.

Although there are exceptions, of course, large flies generally take the larger trout. In Don's opinion, there is still another reason for not using minuscule flies.

"It takes too small a leader for anything that tiny, and I just don't like using a small leader," he says. "You lose too many fish."

The hot July day that I first fished with Don, he was about a third of the way through a book he was writing about fly fishing with the working title of *Tying and Fishing Southern Trout Flies*. After watching him fish, I resolved to be one of the first people in line to purchase his book. There was no doubt that he knew his subject.

All good trout anglers have their favorite flies for fishing North Carolina. Besides the ones that Don mentioned, some other popular North Carolina dry flies include: Humpies, Irresistibles, Rat-faced McDougals, Quill Gordons, Light Cahills (which can also be a wet fly depending on how it is tied), Letort Crickets, and Elk Hair Caddis. Some favorite wet flies, in addition to those mentioned previously in this chapter, include Woolly Worms and Sinking Ants.

Watauga County trout fisherman Roger Caylor, unlike the shoemaker's child, uses flies he makes himself.

When he fishes North Carolina streams, he most often uses the Olive Elk Hair Caddis, the Royal Wulff, the Tellico Nymph, the Pheasant Tail Nymph, the Woolly Bugger, and the Muddler Minnow.

Roger, like Don Howell, has made a name (see Chapters One and Eight) for himself in the fly-tying business.

One other fly rod lure needs mentioning: streamers, which imitate minnows. They can be effective at times.

Photo by Leger Meyland

Flies tied by Roger Caylor. Top: Pheasant Tail Nymph, a wet fly, left; Elk Hair Caddis, a dry fly, right; Middle: Tellico Nymph, a wet fly, left; Woolly Bugger, a wet fly usually classified as a streamer, right. Bottom: Roy Wulff, a dry fly.

Typical streamer, a good fly for big trout. It also will catch other kinds of fish that hit minnows. Paul Salazar ties it especially for crappie.

Photo by Buck Paysour

"They're good for big fish," says John Baskervill. "I fish them about every way I can figure to fish them: fast, slow, on top, and down deep."

Chapter Eight

Turning Mud into Trout

When we telephoned to check, the New River was clear, boding well for our smallmouth-bass fishing trip the next morning. But when we arrived in the mountains, we drove over much of Ashe and Watauga counties without finding any water that looked clear enough to fish. Rain had fallen in some parts of Western North Carolina during the night, washing mud into the river and turning it murky red.

We could see a few rocks, dark shadows, under the water at one stretch of the South Fork of the New River and thought that spot might offer a possibility. We piled out of the car, and John Baskervill quickly pulled on his chest waders, walked upstream a short distance, and eased himself into the river.

Bill Black entered the river next.

But before I could get into my gear, John yelled.

"It's no good," he boomed.

When John makes a judgment about fishing, you don't question him. As mentioned in this book earlier, no other fly fisherman with whom I am acquainted knows more about as many kinds of North Carolina fly fishing—from the mountains to the coast—than he does. Even though he denies it.

111

So the three of us climbed back into Bill's station wagon and drove around the twisting mountain roads to inspect a couple other reaches of the river. All were muddy.

We finally shed our vests and waders and drove to the village of Todd to eat lunch at the Todd General Store. If you have never visited Todd and the store, you should. Both the store and the community have character and visiting them is, as the cliché goes, like stepping back into time.

Todd is a place you might not visit if you did not fish in areas off the beaten track. It is a pleasant mountain community on the Watauga and Ashe County line. It was once a prosperous town with timber providing much of the wealth. A railroad served the town, hauling out timber and other wood products and bringing in passengers and the necessities of life. In its heyday Todd boasted a bank, two hotels, a dentist, four doctors, four churches, nine stores, and even a Ford dealership.

Then the Great Depression hit and the timber business dried up. The town never recovered, and that is not such a bad thing. If it were larger and more developed, it would not be as charming as it is.

Today, two country stores are about all there are to remind you of the long-ago boom times. But the settlement remains wealthy in other more important ways. It is picturesque and the people are friendly, and it is a pleasant place to take a break after a morning of fishing in the South Fork of the New River, which flows by the foot of the village.

Like the village for which it is named, the Todd General Store has personality. It is as you imagine a country store at the turn of the century would have been.

Joe Morgan runs the store. He and his wife, Sheila, came to the North Carolina mountains from their native California in the early 1980s. Joe first engaged in the real estate business. But all the time he sold real estate, he dreamed of some day owning a country store. Then he and Sheila discovered the Todd General Store, which had operated off and on since it was built in 1914 but had been closed for a short while when Joe found it. The Morgans, who are friendly enough to be mistaken for mountain natives, bought the store and reopened it.

They posted signs on the main highways that by-pass Todd, welcoming tourists to the store. And many stop to visit. The Morgans also added antiques and other touches to make the store more attractive to sightseers.

But this is no ersatz country store for the benefit of wayfarers. In fact, most of the store's customers are neighborly mountain folk who live in and around Todd.

Remove your fishing vest and waders and drop by the store on a typical summer day, as we did, and you'll see what it's like. A local woman with young children comes in to buy groceries.

"You mind putting this on my bill?" she says to Joe Morgan, who scribbles a record of the purchase in a pad.

Next, a local man dressed in overalls buys some chewing tobacco for Morgan to duly record on his credit pad.

Then several tourists come to order lunch and, as they settle into rustic booths in the back, Joe whips up sandwiches.

The store sells everything that local folk would need to survive if they were snowbound a week or so, which sometimes happens in these parts.

Included in the stock are overalls and other clothing, spark plugs and other parts for automobiles, trucks and tractors, jellies, canned goods, homemade bread, cream separators, churns, wood-bark bird houses, homemade candy, tin-can lanterns, hand-carved toys, groceries, and antiques of many kinds.

The Morgans also sell the real necessities of life: some very beautiful flies tied by Roger Caylor (see Chapters One and Seven) who lives up the road a piece from the store.

"Hardly a day goes by that I don't sell some flies," Joe says.

We ordered hot dogs and country ham sandwiches. While Joe was preparing our food, we left to assess a nearby spot in the river that John hoped might be clear enough to fish.

It wasn't, and we returned to the store to eat our waiting food.

Bill and John, after a brief conference, decided to give up on smallmouth bass—at least for this day.

"What would you say about trying a little trout fishing?" John asked.

Bill and I said that was fine. I was especially happy; I would get an opportunity to fish for mountain trout with John—something I had long wanted to do.

We drove a few miles to a small, pretty white church beside a small brook, which was crystal clear. Bill parked the station wagon, and John and Bill put on their hip boots. They usually carry those, along with their waders, on fishing trips to the mountains. I put my waders back on and resolved to pack my hip boots the next time I went small-mouth bass fishing—in case I should again end up fishing for trout instead of bass.

Luckily, I had brought along one light fly rod but no trout flies. Bill loaned me a dry fly, an Adams. John waded off in one direction. I went in another. Bill soon came behind me and caught several brook trout in stretches of water that I had already fished.

114

After about an hour, John came back to the church yard where we had parked Bill's station wagon. He reported that he had caught brown, brook and rainbows.

The stream was a narrow one and was, according to the North Carolina Wildlife Resources Commission sign on the bridge, a hatchery-supported stream. That meant that a tank truck came by from time to time and seeded the stream with trout.

John next guided us to another stream that he had fished many times. (There are not many that John has not fished). At the new stream, Bill and John caught fish, and I had several rises.

"Let's go up a little way and we'll see how to really catch trout," John said.

We got back into the station wagon and drove about a mile.

"Why don't you park right here?" John suggested, pointing to a place where we could get all the way off the road.

John's leader had separated from his line. Rather than repair it, he decided to let us do most of the fishing. He suggested that Bill and I switch to larger dry flies.

"You can see them better," he said.

Bill quickly did as John suggested and also loaned me a larger dry fly, a Size Ten Yellow Humpy.

After we had entered the stream and had waded only a short distance, John pointed to a riffle and told Bill, "Flip your fly right there and let it wash around."

Bill did as John suggested. His fly danced on the swift water only a second before it disappeared. Bill landed a trout, a rainbow, that put up a valiant struggle for its modest size. No wonder—this was, as were all the trout in this reach of the stream, a native or "wild" trout: a trout that was spawned and grew up where Bill caught it, as opposed to being stocked there.

The narrow stream provided room for only one person to fish, so Bill and I "leap-frogged," or took turns going ahead to fish water that John indicated. I got a rise at the first place that John suggested but missed the fish. On my second attempt, I had better luck and landed a scrappy rainbow.

It was like that the rest of the afternoon. Almost every time John advised us to do something, trout rose to our flies, and we hooked and landed most of them.

In one pool at the bottom of a riffle, a rainbow seemed to come out of nowhere to rise to my Humpy. It missed the hook but seized the hackle and tugged the fly under the water, quickly turning it loose. Then we saw it come back to nail the fly again before the fly had time to bounce back to the surface of the water. This time, I caught the trout.

John occasionally borrowed one of our rods to make a cast, always catching trout.

The reach of the creek that we fished was never more than knee deep. It was narrow, rarely more than ten feet wide and was overgrown with bushes. Sometimes we fished under bushes that hung just inches off the water. But it didn't matter. We caught fish in many places where only our leaders and none of our fly lines were in the water. In other places all it took were short roll casts to reach the spots that John counseled us to fish. It was "short-lining" at its best.

"You see what I mean when I say it's easier to catch trout than to catch bass on a fly rod," John said, repeating a comment he often makes, a comment that irritates some of his fly fishing friends.

The trout were easy to catch, all right. But the fishing was more strenuous than any bass fishing I have ever done. We often had to climb high banks beside the stream and pick our way around obstacles. At other places we had to crawl, like mountain goats, over boulders, or creep across slick underwater stones. We walked through culverts and bent our backs to make our way under bridges.

At the end of the day's fishing, we were tired and sweaty, but happy.

Bill kept talking about how lucky we were to have received tutoring on "short-lining" from John.

"He's a master," Bill said.

"You're pretty good yourself," I said.

"I'm a novice compared to John," Bill said.

Who isn't? I thought.

None of the trout we caught were huge. But when I stopped to read the plaque on a bridge that told us that this was a wild trout stream and specified size limits, I realized that every trout we caught had been big enough to keep. We had released them all.

When we stopped in North Wilkesboro to eat dinner on the way home, I recalled how disappointed I had been when we found the New River to be too muddy for smallmouth bass fishing.

But the day had turned out to be anything but disappointing.

"John," I said, "you turned lemons into lemonade."

If I had been real clever, I would have said that John turned mud into trout.

Photo by Steve Brown

Vince Davis with big brown trout.

Chapter Nine

Tar Heel Trout Fishing: It's Different

Bill Wilkerson is a fortunate fly fisherman.

He is an airline pilot, which means that he can fly free to some of world's best trout fishing waters, and he does that regularly.

But for Bill, distance does not necessarily lend enchantment. He still enjoys fishing for mountain trout right in his own home state of North Carolina.

"Our streams do not hold the number of trout that some other waters hold," he says. "But North Carolina has some quality trout fishing, and the state's trout fishing has a special charm and beauty."

Bill believes that fishing for trout in North Carolina is more challenging than in many other states.

"In Montana, for example, where the water is more open, I've seen fly fishermen standing two abreast," he says. "They often will stand in the same spot and cast a half day—and catch fish. You seldom see that in our state or in neighboring states. Most Appalachian trout fly fishing is not like that shown in the movie *A River Runs Through It*, which depicts anglers making long casts.

"The Appalachian style of fishing usually involves short casts because most streams are small and have obstructions

Photo by Bill Wilkerson

John Baskervill fishing for trout on mountain stream.

instead of being wide and open as are many western rivers. In addition, we do not have as many long smooth flats. We have faster running waters, more riffles."

Bill says many anglers from western states who come to North Carolina try to fish the same way they fish at home: long casts with a lot of false casting.

"That often spooks the fish," Bill says.

Besides, anglers who try to make long casts while fishing North Carolina streams often get snagged on bushes, briars, trees, and other such things that are behind them or over their heads.

Don Howell agrees that North Carolina trout fishing is more difficult.

"I'd put a good fly fisherman from North Carolina up against fly fishermen from any other state any time," Don says.

Although it is difficult and often unnecessary to make long fly casts on many North Carolina trout streams, they may be required when the water is low and clear.

"I'd rather cast into a pool than slip up to it," Bill says. "But the traditional Appalachian style of fishing involves more poking around in pockets with a short line and a short leader."

Even when casting into a pool, Bill prefers making short casts when possible.

John Baskervill thinks the same way.

"A lot of the times, you don't even have to cast to catch trout," he says. "And hardly ever do you have to make long casts."

In fact, John says, he seldom makes long casts and sometimes he fishes all day with only his leader touching the water.

"You are going to lose a lot of fish on a long cast," he explains. "You have a hard time setting the hook because you've got all that slack line and elasticity of the line and spring of the rod. Short casts are better no matter what kind of fish you are fishing for: trout, bass, bream and so forth. When I see somebody out making those long beautiful casts on a stream, I know I'm going to beat him—or her."

North Carolina trout fishing is different in still another way.

"In many other states, some people fish the hatches and only the hatches," Bill Wilkerson says. "We don't have that in North Carolina."

Hatches, of course, occur when insects become airborne after emerging from their nymph or larva stage. Then they swarm over a stream and fall into the water, usually causing trout to feed on the surface. In states that have huge hatches, anglers spend much time trying to "match the hatch" or trying to find or create flies that duplicate the insects involved in hatches.

But this is usually a waste of time in North Carolina. John Baskervill and his son, Robert, were once wading and fishing Basin Creek near Elkin when they spotted two fly fishermen sitting on a big boulder and staring patiently across the water. It was about noon.

"They were dressed like what I call 'yuppie fishermen,' " John recalls. "Their vests bulged with flies and other para-phernalia."

"Catching anything?" John asked.

"Not yet," replied one of the yuppie fishermen. "We're waiting for the hatch."

The first time I fished with Don Howell, I told him that story.

Chuckling, he said, "Those fisherman probably had a long wait."

Some North Carolina trout streams do have a few hatches. But they are unimportant when compared to hatches that occur in some other states.

"We don't try to match the hatch specifically," Don Howell said. "Your fly just makes a silhouette to the trout anyway."

Even if North Carolina doesn't have hatches and even if some other states have trout waters that are easier to fish, Bill Wilkerson thinks the state's trout fishing is unsurpassed in several ways.

"We have some of the best traditional wild trout fishing in the country," he declares.

Wild trout are native trout: fish that live their lives in the stream in which they are born—as opposed to hatchery fish that are stocked in a stream.

"It's a joy to land a wild trout," Bill says.

Bill loves North Carolina trout fishing for other reasons, and you can tell from the tenor of his voice that he would just as soon not dwell on whether our fishing is as good as that of other states.

"To compare North Carolina fishing with other places is like talking about apples and oranges," he says. "North Carolina may not have quite as good trout fishing as some other states, but it can afford an angler a lifetime of fine fishing."

Don Howell says much the same thing.

Like Bill, he has fished for trout in many places: Montana, Wyoming, Idaho and several other western states, and in Alaska and Canada.

But ask him which state he would choose if he had to pick just one, and he will answer, "North Carolina. Absolutely."

North Carolina has plenty of trout water to fish.

More than a fourth of the state's one hundred counties have some trout fishing.

The counties in which you can find at least some trout streams include: Alexander, Alleghany, Ashe, Avery, Buncombe, Burke, Caldwell, Cherokee, Clay, Graham, Haywood, Henderson, Jackson, Macon, Madison, McDowell, Mitchell, Polk, Rutherford, Stokes, Surry, Swain, Transylvania, Watauga, Wilkes, and Yancey.

The South Toe River, especially known for its big brown trout, is Don Howell's second favorite place to fish—second only to his beloved Davidson River.

He also likes the Elk River and the Linville River and all the Smoky Mountain trout streams.

Some other good North Carolina trout streams include portions of Bradley Fork Creek, Bullhead Creek, Deep Creek, Harper Creek, Hazel Creek, Nantahala River, Santeetlah River, Whitewater River, and Wilson Creek, to name just a few (see Appendix F).

In fact, you can sometimes catch trout just by driving around and exploring. You stop your car at any likely looking stream and fish. Using this method of finding trout streams is like the man who was standing on the street asking for a kiss from every pretty woman who passed by.

"Don't you get your face slapped a lot doing that?" a passerby asked.

"Yeah," replied the man. "But you'd be surprised how many kisses I get."

You might not catch any fish at some of the streams you pick at random. But you might be surprised how many times you do catch fish.

But you should be very careful, especially when you fish streams in remote areas that you have never fished before. It is easy to get lost after you have waded a stream for a while. If you are not familiar with the stream, one place looks much like others, especially late in the day when shadows can play tricks on you. I have known trout fishermen who were forced to spend the night in the woods because they could not find the trails that they came in on.

Bill Black thinks one of the reasons North Carolina trout fishing can sometimes be so good is that our trout are often hungry.

"There isn't as much food in our streams as there is in some of the western streams," he says.

One thing that appeals to me about North Carolina trout fishing is that it is often uncrowded.

"North Carolina trout fishing is one of the best-kept secrets there is," Don Howell says. "When you fish in Montana, say, and meet somebody who has never fished for trout in North Carolina, and they find out that you are from North Carolina, they'll say something like, 'You don't have any trout fishing in your state, do you?' It suits me just fine if our trout fishing remains a secret."

Some of the state's very best trout streams empty into deep mountain lakes. You can also catch trout on a fly rod in the lakes themselves. When fishing mountain lakes for trout, many fly rod anglers use deep-sinking lines or at least streamers that sink deep on their own. Generally speaking, you should use larger flies or streamers when fishing for trout in lakes.

125

You might also catch some smallmouth bass or even largemouth bass (see Chapters Four and Six) while fishing for trout in lakes. Or you might do the opposite: catch trout while fishing for bass.

Just one more word about the question: Which is the most difficult to catch on a fly rod, bass or mountain trout?

I asked that question of another fly fisherman I admire: Vince Davis of Lewisville.

There seemed to be no doubt in his mind: bass are the most perplexing.

"At least that's been my experience," he says. "I can go out and catch trout most any day. That's not true of bass, even though I have had some great days fishing for largemouth bass."

Vince had been using a fly rod for only about nine years when I met him, but he had already become an accomplished fly fisherman. Although Vince had long been an avid outdoorsman and began fishing with other types of gear when he was just a little boy—his father took him often—he did not discover fly fishing until he was an adult.

It was a bit of misfortune that led Vince to the fly rod.

Tendonitis put an end to his rock climbing, which had been one of his most enjoyable past-times.

"After developing tendonitis, I started hiking instead of rock climbing," he says.

A hiking trip to Stone Mountain Park changed his life. He stopped beside a stream to watch a small brown trout that was sipping bugs off the top of the water.

"I thought 'Gee, I need to figure out how to catch fish such as that one.' "

That led him to take up fly fishing. Since then, he has fly fished over much of North Carolina and portions of

Tennessee. He has caught many species of fish on a fly rod, including crappie, catfish, white bass, smallmouth bass, striped bass, largemouth bass, mountain trout and cypress trout (another name for bowfin).

He lives in Lewisville, west of Winston-Salem, which makes it handy for him to run to Wilkes County to fish for trout.

The tendonitis that led him to take up fly fishing not only changed his life but also that of his father, Robert Davis.

Vince talked his dad into trying the fly rod. Now Robert loves fly fishing almost as much as his son does.

And that is a lot.

Vince not only fishes often, but he also makes his own beautiful fly rods and ties many of his own flies. He originated one fly that he called the "In-Vince-A-Beetle." It has a body of spun deer hair with an outer body of coated turkey quill and trimmed hackle feathers for legs.

The In-Vince-A-Beetle is almost impossible to sink. It will float even after you have caught dozens of trout on it. It is especially potent in warm weather, reaching its peak effectiveness in August and September in a normal year.

If it is true that trout are easier to catch than are bass, one of the reasons may be that trout streams are less subject to the vagaries of the weather than are bass waters.

Photo by Bill Cleveland

John Baskervill with speckled sea trout caught on a fly on
White Oak River near Swansboro.

Chapter Ten

Trout With a Taste of Salt

It is summer and the water is warm. Hubert Parrott is "wading wet," or in shorts and tennis shoes instead of in waders or hip boots. He is fishing a nine-foot fly rod and a nine-weight floating line.

He strips line from his reel, makes a false cast, then shoots his fly—a streamer—about twenty-five feet. He lets his streamer settle in the water before beginning his retrieve by stripping in line.

He is fishing for trout. Only the water in which he is fishing is much different than the mountain streams that Don Howell usually fishes. So are the trout.

Hubert is fishing for saltwater trout: speckled trout, also known as spotted trout, speckled sea trout, sea trout or just plain "specks."

Sometimes, Hubert will fish from his boat. But today, he has pulled his skiff up into the marsh so he can wade and fish.

"I like to wade when I can," he explains. "It's fun and it's comfortable, especially in the summer."

Today, as he often does, he is fishing near Swansboro within sight of his home. The picturesque house sits on a knoll and he and his wife, Cotten, can sit on their sun porch and sip coffee while enjoying a spectacular view of the White Oak River. In front of their home, the river forms a large bay as it pauses to rest before flowing into Bogue Sound about twenty miles south of Morehead City.

Hubert fishes the White Oak for trout most of the year, or until it is so cold that he can't stand it. In the relatively mild climate of the area, that means he fishes all but a few weeks each year. Although he catches his biggest trout in the fall, his favorite time to fish is in the spring and summer. He likes that time because it is usually the least crowded time. Area farmers, many of whom are avid speckled trout fishermen, are too busy tending crops to fish.

When Hubert gets the urge to go fishing and can find time away from his work—he commutes about fifty miles to Kinston where he is in the insurance business—all he has to do is walk down to his dock, climb in his modest eighteen-foot skiff, crank the motor and run to the spot where he thinks he might find trout.

But finding them is often difficult.

"Just when you think you have them figured out, when you expect them to be in a certain place, they won't be there," he says. "That's the challenge of it. I love to hunt, and I think fishing for trout is about as much hunting as it is fishing."

He searches for trout around bridge and pier pilings, over shell beds, rocks, and other such places.

"They are like largemouth bass in that respect," he says. "They like to hang around stuff."

Hubert prefers to fish areas that have moving water.

He sometimes starts out with spinning or baitcasting gear. Then, when he catches trout, he changes to his fly rod. If he concludes that conditions are not right for fly fishing, he will forsake the long rod in favor of other types of equipment. This happens most often in the winter, when the fish are in deep water.

Speckled trout, particularly big ones, are hard to catch on a fly rod, especially when they are in deep water.

One year, Hubert caught fewer than a half dozen. But in other years, he has done very well. He once caught seven fish on seven casts.

Occasionally, a fly rod will even outfish other types of gear. On those rare times, trout will wallop a fly rod lure when they will only toy with a spinning or baitcasting lure. This is most likely to happen when the fish are in shallow water.

"Sometimes they will nudge a topwater lure such as a Mirrolure but not take it," Hubert says.

When fish do that, he quickly switches to his fly rod and uses a popper similar to a bass bug and fishes it just about the way he fishes a bass bug for largemouth bass.

"A lot of times, trout will grab the bug as soon as it hits the water," Hubert says. "I believe the fish think the bug is a skipping shrimp. You've seen shrimp dancing across the surface of the water."

When fly fishing for speckled trout, Hubert seldom fishes a fly deeper than nine feet under the surface of the water, and he rarely fishes a fast sinking line or even a sink tip line.

"I'd rather for the weight to be on the fly," he says.

That's why the Clouser Minnow—a fast-sinking streamer—is one of his favorites for trout when he has to go under the water. Sometimes, if the trout are deep but turn up their noses at the Clouser Minnow, he'll use a streamer that doesn't sink fast on its own and attach a split shot to his leader to get the streamer deep.

But on some days, a fly rod angler doesn't have to worry about all that.

"I can't emphasize too much to anybody who wants to try this that they often don't have to fish deep water," he says. "I would say that ninety percent of the trout that I have caught on a fly rod have been caught in water that was shallow enough to wade in. But it is better to fish shallow water either early or late in the day or on an overcast day. Trout don't like a lot of bright light."

Hubert owns and has used many types of fly line: floating, sinking, sink tip, shooting taper, and so on. But his favorite is a weight-forward, neutral-buoyancy line that was designed primarily for bonefishing. When not dressed with floatant, the line sinks, but very slowly.

Hubert ties his own tapered leaders, usually using thirty-pound test monofilament for the butt section, a middle section of fifteen- to eighteen-pound test, and ten-pound test for the tippet. Occasionally, he will use eight-pound test for the tippet. He coats the knots with clear fingernail polish to strengthen them and to make them smoother.

As in other types of fly fishing, a good rule of thumb for sea trout fishing is that a leader should be about the length of your rod. This, of course, can be lengthened or shortened depending on fishing conditions.

Hubert has a fine collection of fly rods of various weights and lengths that he keeps rigged so that he can go fishing at a moment's notice. He has used all of the rods.

Most of the time, though, he fishes a nine footer matched for an eight-weight or nine-weight line.

"You can usually catch a trout on the same outfit you use for largemouth bass," he says. "I have used a rod as heavy as a twelve-weight (matched for a twelve-weight line) when I needed something to throw into a stiff wind. But it's just not much fun to catch a trout on that."

Hubert's favorite flies include the popper, the Clouser Minnow, the Lefty's Deceiver, and the Charlie, a bonefish fly that looks a lot like a shrimp.

"I've also caught them on junk that I've tied myself, things that don't look like anything that I've ever seen," he says. "If it's got some sparkle in it, it'll catch fish. But I've probably caught more trout on the Charlie than anything else."

He was using a Charlie the day he caught seven trout on seven casts.

He favors flies that have lead eyes like those on many of the Charlie patterns.

He usually fishes sinking flies by retrieving in short strips, making the fly dart to simulate bait fish.

"If you've got a good current, it will do most of the work for you," he says.

He believes a beginner who is interested in catching sea trout should start off fishing for other saltwater species that are easier to catch. Bluefish (see Chapter Fourteen) is one of the species he recommends for this.

If you do take up fly fishing for sea trout, you'll be joining an exclusive fraternity. A few fly rod anglers (including my friend John Baskervill) do it occasionally, but not many do it often. Hubert is personally acquainted with only one other person who regularly fishes for sea trout with a fly rod. The other person is Courtney Humphrey of Kinston, who got Hubert started in the sport.

Hubert catches several varieties of saltwater fish and, when he gets far enough upstream to reach brackish water, even some freshwater fish. But trout are his first love.

"There is no fish that is any prettier," he says. "They are almost too pretty to kill."

Sea trout share something in common with the mountain trout. Like mountain trout, they are delicious, something which has contributed to the decline of the colorful and beautiful fish. Many people who farm or hold other jobs in Onslow and neighboring counties fish commercially for trout on the White Oak River in their spare time.

Sports anglers worked to get limits on the sizes and numbers of trout that may be kept. So you should check the latest regulations before fishing for trout if you plan to keep any. Hubert now releases most of those he catches, occasionally keeping only enough for one meal.

"It's fun to catch a trout on a fly rod and turn it loose while somebody is in a nearby boat fishing with other equipment," he says. "I pick the trout up, look at it, then release it. I've had people call me all kinds of S.O.B. for doing that. They say, 'Don't throw another one overboard. If you catch another one, I want it.' "

But they never get their wants from Hubert.

John Rucker, a Greensboro construction contractor, became interested in fly fishing for sea trout by accident.

"I just decided to try it," he says.

Through trial and error, he learned the same basic lessons that Hubert Parrott has learned. Now when conditions are right, John fishes for speckled trout with a fly rod.

But, like Hubert, John has concluded that there are times when it is foolish to try to use the fly rod for trout. So, also like Hubert, John will often abandon the fly rod in favor of other equipment.

When he does fly fish for sea trout, John employs similar methods, similar equipment and similar flies to those that Hubert uses.

John fishes in the inlets and other sheltered waters of southeastern North Carolina.

"I just don't think it is very practical to fish in the surf with a fly rod," he says.

Fortunately, however, sea trout do sometimes haunt relatively sheltered waters, both salt and brackish, that are ideal for fly fishing with relatively light gear.

Some of these waters include tributaries to the Pamlico Sound and streams that flow into those tributaries. Among these streams are Goose Creek (the one that flows into the Pamlico River), North Creek, Pungo Creek, sheltered stretches of the Pungo River, and South Creek; Germanton Bay and Juniper Bay; some sheltered portions of the Neuse River and tributaries to the Neuse including, but not necessarily restricted to, Bay River, Goose Creek (different from the Goose Creek mentioned above), Jones Bay, North River, South River, Upper Broad Creek, and similar waters.

Other waters that could be fished with a fly rod and which sometimes hold trout include relatively sheltered portions of Hubert's White Oak River, Queens Creek (a tributary to the White Oak River), and the Newport River, among others. Some tributaries to the Albemarle Sound are also excellent for fly fishing for speckled trout.

Photo by Leger Meyland

Tom Kirkman with striped bass caught on a fly rod while fishing turbulent waters beneath dam.

Chapter Eleven

Stripers and Hybrids

Tom Kirkman was standing in a boat that was rocking furiously, yet he managed to make a decent cast with his nine-foot, ten-weight fly rod. The streamer at the end of his ten-pound test leader tippet fell into the churning water close to the concrete dam that towered above the boat.

Tom let the streamer sink below the water's surface for a moment and began his retrieve. He had stripped in only a few feet of line when he felt an abrupt jolt that he thought would rip the fly rod from his hand.

The fight was on: man against strong fish, fish and the elements against man and graphite and metal and plastic. For a while, there was a question about who would win. Tom had to keep the fish away from the concrete of the dam and away from the boulders that littered the tumbling water below the dam. Finally after a battle of about a half hour, during which the boat continued to shudder so much that Tom had to plant his feet wide apart to keep his balance, the fish surrendered.

Although exhausted, Tom immediately made another cast.

He could not believe what happened.

There was a jolt similar to the one he had felt on the previous cast. The battle that followed seemed even more fierce than the first. Or maybe it was just that the first fish had so fatigued Tom.

After another long interval, Tom won this battle too.

His partner, Wayne McGinnis, grinned. Wayne had reason to be happy. After all, he had introduced Tom to this kind of fishing.

Today, the two striped bass that Tom caught on back-to-back casts hang on the wall of his High Point shop where he can look at them and relive the battles when he takes a break from tying flies and making and repairing fishing rods.

The fish, each weighing more than thirteen pounds, are beautiful striped bass. If you have ever caught even a moderate-size striper on heavy tackle, you know how strong they are. You also can imagine how much sport it would be to land one on a fly rod.

If Wayne McGinnis had not had to retire from the State Highway Patrol after injuring his back, Tom might never have started fly fishing for striped bass. At least it would have taken him longer to discover the sport.

Tom recalls, "After Wayne hurt his back, somebody took him down to Badin Lake. Wayne, using spinning tackle, caught an eleven-pound striper on his first cast. That did it. That fish has cost him more than $50,000. He had to have a boat. Then he had to have something to pull the boat with. Then he had to have a house closer to the lake. Then he had to have...."

In the mid-1980s, Wayne invited Tom to go striper fishing, and Tom caught a couple of stripers on spinning tackle. That did it with Tom. He had to have....

After Wayne introduced Tom to striper fishing, the two anglers began fishing the tail races below hydroelectric and flood control dams. Tom, who had long been a lover of fly fishing, soon observed something about fishing in the tumbling water below dams.

"I thought the areas would be perfect for shallow-water fly fishing for striped bass," he says.

So he took his fly rod along on a trip and caught his first striper on a fly rod. Since then he has landed many of the big, beautiful, hard-fighting, and long-running fish on fly rods. He has caught them on a fly rod in the swift waters below the dams of lakes such as Badin, Falls of the Neuse, Kerr Lake, Tuckertown, and others.

He also has caught them on a fly rod in the lakes above the dams and in the shallow, brackish waters of the Alligator River and other Eastern North Carolina creeks, rivers and sounds.

Much of what he has learned through experience can help any fly fisherman who wants to try fishing for striped bass—no matter where he fishes.

But he has some special advice about fishing below dams, advice that has nothing to do with catching fish. The advice could save your life.

"It's dangerous water," he says of the areas. "You are not going to get a chance to make two mistakes."

The only practical way for a fly fisherman to fish these waters is from a boat because there are not many places where you can fish from shore. And the few places where you can fish from land are often crowded with fishermen using casting and spinning equipment, making fly fishing next to impossible.

"Fly fishermen just do not fit into that setting," Tom observes.

But the water that rushes down from lakes above the dams is not especially suitable for boat fishing, either. You need to be very cautious.

"You've got some real shallow and rocky areas," Tom says. "It's real treacherous."

The water is particularly menacing when flood gates of the dam are flung open. There is often little or no warning before this happens. So how does the angler tell when the gates are about to open?

"You just have to be observant," Tom says.

He has seen boats demolished as currents battered them against rocks. Sometimes, the rushing water wedges boats against the rocks, and there is no escape until the crescendo subsides.

In a typical year, spring is the time when flood gates must be frequently disengaged to release water. Spring also happens to be one of the two times when striped bass fishing below dams is best. Fall is the other time.

"Those are the times when striped bass run up into the rivers and congregate below the dams," says Tom.

For striper fishing below the dams, Tom, who makes his own rods, likes a nine-foot rod matched for a Number Ten line.

"That's an ideal outfit, particularly if you get into stripers that weigh over ten pounds each—something that is not hard to do," Tom says. "Sure, you can catch stripers on seven- or eight-weight gear when you have open water. But below dams, you seldom have that. Then there are the rocks that you have to contend with, and you've also got to fight the current when you fish below dams."

Tom prefers to use a multiplier reel, one that retrieves more than one turn of line with each turn of the handle, for striper fishing with a fly outfit. But he has difficulty finding multiplying reels with reliable drags. So he usually uses single action reels with good disk drags.

One reason it is important to chose your reel with care is that you have to fight stripers from the reel.

"You won't strip many stripers in by hand," Tom says.

He uses backing to fill his reel. This serves two purposes (see Chapter One). First, a full reel gives him a little more leverage than he would have with a partially loaded reel and, second, the backing gives him plenty of line to fight a striper, which just about always takes out more than his fly line.

Tom prefers twenty-pound test backing, but some people use thirty-pound because it takes less line to fill a reel and is therefore more economical.

"Typically, when a fish breaks off, it breaks off at the leader and not at the backing," he says. "So any backing that is stronger than your leader will serve the purpose."

Speaking of leaders, Tom generally uses ten- or twelve-pound test tippets.

"I don't want to say stripers are leader shy," he says. "But I do know that once you get above about ten- or twelve-pound test your strikes drop off tremendously. But if you go below ten-pound test tippets, you are not going to land many stripers."

To make his leaders less visible, Tom camouflages them by tinting them green with a Magic Marker pen.

"If you do this, you can use a twelve-pound test leader and get as many strikes as you get on eight-pound that has not been tinted," he says. "That's a trick people should use no matter what species they are fishing for."

Tom likes to use green line even when he is fishing for stripers with spinning equipment or live bait. But then, of

Photo by Leger Meyland

Deceiver streamer flies of type used by Tom Kirkman for catching stripers. These are also effective for fishing in brackish water and salt water.

course, he buys line that has the green built in to the line. It would be impractical to tint that much line.

For the fly line itself, Tom favors a bass bug or saltwater taper. It helps him throw large striper flies into the wind. He almost always uses floating line and a sinking fly when fishing for stripers. On a rare occasion, he will use a sink-tip line—one that sinks the first few feet.

"But a floating line is pretty versatile," he says. "By varying the length of leader and the type fly, you can get down a little way. For example, if you use a seven-and-a-half-foot leader and a Lefty's Deceiver or a Clouser Minnow or something else that has weight to it, it is going to drop down several feet. You don't want to get much deeper than that when you are fishing the tail races. Most of those areas are so rocky that you are just going to stay hung up all the time if you go much deeper."

He also likes the Chico's Bendback streamer, especially for fishing rocks or weeds because its hook rides upside down. This keeps the streamer from getting snagged as much as do some other streamers.

Tom uses the same techniques no matter what dam he fishes.

"The situation you have is almost identical regardless of what dam you go below," he says.

In the tail races, just as in the in the weed-strewn waters of Eastern North Carolina, the fly rod has at least one advantage over other types of fishing gear.

"With casting or spinning tackle, once you throw it out, you've got to bring it all the way back in," Tom points out. "You've got to come through the rocks or whatever may be between you and the fish. With a fly rod, you can throw your lure out fifty or sixty feet, casting over the rocks or weeds. Then, on your retrieve, you can lift your fly over the rocks or weeds and cast back out again."

Tom tries to cast against the current. Then he strips in line at about the same speed as the current.

"I guess what I do is to let the current move the fly while I take the slack out," he says.

Usually, long casts are not necessary. However, landing a striper on fly tackle—something that is tricky under the best of circumstances—is especially challenging in the tail races.

"It's a strange fight," says Tom.

The fisherman has both boulders and concrete to foil him. The concrete is especially mean.

"Once your leader touches the concrete," Tom says, "that's the end of the game."

The leader parts as if you had run a hacksaw through it.

When fishing below dams, an angler has to figure out a way to let the swift current work for him. Also, with experience, an angler learns how much pressure his rod and leader will take.

Stripers move around a lot; therefore you do not usually find them in tail races all day long.

"But typically, they are going to be in there at some time during the day," Tom says.

When fishing inland lakes or Eastern North Carolina brackish waters for stripers, Tom uses about the same flies and the same methods that he uses in the tail races. Except, of course, he doesn't have to contend with swift currents.

And although he loves catching fish on a fly rod, he will use spinning or baitcasting tackle when stripers are down deep.

"If the fish are thirty feet down," he says, "it's just not very conducive to using a fly rod."

Still he prefers the fly rod when possible.

"It's just more fun than any other kind of tackle," he says. "And if you are proficient and the conditions are right, it can be just as productive as spinning and baitcasting tackle."

The ideal time to use a fly rod is when stripers are near the surface or schooling on the surface. But even then, Tom almost always uses a sinking fly rather than a floating one.

"A popper is the least effective fly there is," he says. "I know that when stripers are schooling on top, you can catch some that way. But it's like the difference in fishing a Hula Popper or a plastic worm for largemouth bass. The Hula Popper is fun. But you'll usually catch more fish on the plastic worm.

"If you see a school of stripers on top, typically there will be another school of larger ones below the surface school. The small ones on top will bust shad and kill them, and a lot of those shad will drop down and the big stripers will be there, waiting to eat the shad.

"Then, if you fish with a sink tip line or some other thing to get below the surface, you'll often catch bigger fish."

When Tom fishes a sinking fly to surface schools while his partner fishes floating flies, he almost always catches more stripers and larger stripers than does his partner.

"Besides, what happens if you are fishing a popper to a school on top and the fish decide to go down?" he asks, rhetorically. "Then you're out of the game."

Some fly rod anglers solve this problem by keeping two rods in their boat, one rigged with a surface offering and the other with a sinking fly. They do this no matter the species they are fishing for.

Tom sees no need for doing that. He can work his sinking fly near the surface or several feet under the surface by varying the speed of his retrieve.

Incidentally, casting to surface-feeding schools is one of the few times when an angler needs to make long casts.

"The fish are easy to spook then," says Tom. "If you drop something in the wrong place in your boat or make other wrong kinds of noises or get your boat too close, the stripers will go down."

Tom pays attention to small details, no matter what species of fish he is pursuing.

For example, he does not fasten his fly to his leader with a knot that is snug with the eye of the hook. Instead, he uses a loop. This allows his fly to swing free, improving its action.

When he uses spinning or baitcasting equipment, he accomplishes the same thing by using a split ring between the eye of his lure and his line.

"A human can't see the difference in the action this makes, but the fish apparently do," he says.

Tom goes against conventional wisdom in much of his fishing. For example, he believes a fly fisherman should cast and retrieve with the same hand. Many right-handed anglers cast with their right hands and reel with their left when using fly tackle so they won't have to switch their rods from one hand to the other to retrieve their fly or land a fish. Some left-handed anglers cast with their left hand and retrieve with their right for the same reason.

Tom disagrees.

"If you don't switch hands, you will be so tired after you have landed a big fish your arm will feel like rubber and your next cast will be difficult," he explains.

Makes sense if you think about it.

Tom prefers a fly that has a little flash to it. He ties and sells striper flies in his rod-building shop.

"I think the best color is chartreuse with a little bit of gold mixed in, no matter where I'm fishing," he says. "When I've got that color on and I'm not catching fish, I don't blame the fly. I think I just need to wait until some fish move in. Or maybe I need to move to where the fish are."

But he doesn't think the color of a fly is as important as is the confidence with which it is fished.

"Most fishermen will catch more fish if they spend less time changing flies or lures and more time fishing," he points out. "I think it is better to fish your fly in a variety of ways, by changing depth, changing your retrieve, fishing slower or faster, and just waiting the fish out. I just don't see the point in clipping off your fly, changing it, clipping it off and changing it...."

In fact, Tom has found that stripers that are feeding will hit just about any reasonable fly or other lure. But when stripers are not feeding, he says, an angler can throw everything in his tackle box or fly vest at them without getting a sniff.

"A largemouth bass has more personality than a striper," Tom says. "A largemouth will hit because it is angry. But not a striper. It will usually hit only when it is feeding. But when it is feeding, it is not as finicky as a largemouth."

There is another difference in stripers and largemouth bass, says Tom.

"To me, stripers are not nearly as structure-oriented as largemouth bass. Stripers stay on the move more."

There is still another big difference in the striper and many other species of fish. The striper seems to tolerate wretched weather or other conditions that would be considered bad for fishing for other species. In fact, sometimes stripers seem even to prefer bad weather.

When a striper is feeding, Tom says, you can catch it in water so muddy you wonder how it can even see your fly. In muddy water, Tom does like to use a fly that has an abundance of glitter.

For many years, anglers had little opportunity to catch striped bass in inland waters. The reason: Few, if any biologists, thought stripers could survive in fresh water without having access to salt water or at least brackish water. So nobody thought about stocking the fish in fresh water.

It was known, of course, that stripers were anadromous— fish that spend part of their lives in salt or brackish water and part in fresh water, running up into fresh or brackish waters to spawn. Then a serendipitous thing occurred. Dams were built on the Santee-Cooper rivers, trapping stripers in fresh water. Those stripers not only thrived without being able to get to salt water, they also reproduced.

Since then, striped bass have been successfully stocked in many inland waters, including a number of North Carolina lakes. Stripers have flourished in most freshwater lakes in which they have been stocked but reproduce in only a few. Stripers need long rivers in which to migrate to spawn successfully. In North Carolina, Kerr Lake (which is partly in Virginia) is the only freshwater lake where stripers reproduce. I caught my first freshwater striper in that lake. It had been tagged on its spawning run up the Staunton River the year before.

In most freshwater lakes, however, the striper fishery is strictly a put-and-take proposition. Ironically, at the same time freshwater stripers were multiplying, the numbers of their saltwater and brackish-water relatives were drastically declining. They became so rare that some people wondered if they were not in danger of extinction. Pollution and over-fishing by both commercial and sports fishermen were blamed.

In recent years, Eastern North Carolina saltwater and brackish-water stripers have made a dramatic comeback, thanks to the conservation efforts of the North Carolina Wildlife Resources Commission and other governmental agencies.

The agencies have, from time to time, limited the size and number of striped bass that can be legally kept, put in other restrictions, stocked fish, and taken additional steps to improve striper populations.

Now, almost every time I fish the Alligator River, a tributary to the Albemarle Sound, I see several schools of stripers slashing minnows on the surface. For fifteen years or so, that was a rare sight.

Spotting a big school of stripers is exciting. But even when they are not schooling on top, they usually travel in packs.

"If you catch one striper, there are usually more there," says Tom Kirkman. "He is not swimming by himself."

Stanley Winbourne of Raleigh (see Chapter Fourteen) sometimes uses his fly rod to catch a fish that some people might mistake for a striped bass or a big white bass.

Little wonder that the uninitiated might at first think that the fish is either a striper or a white bass. It looks much like both fish. It fights as ferociously—many anglers say even more ferociously—than a striped bass. It is difficult to say whether it fights better than a white bass, (see Chapter Thirteen) because it grows to be much larger than a white bass.

But this fish shares some of the characteristics of both the white bass and the striped bass. Little wonder. It is the progeny of both, a cross of the two species.

This hybrid bass has been officially proclaimed the "Bodie Bass" in North Carolina in honor of my friend Bodie McDowell, former outdoors editor of the Greensboro *News & Record*, for his conservation efforts.

The Bodie Bass is usually produced in a hatchery by using the striped bass for a mama and a white bass for a papa. Occasionally, a hybrid can occur naturally—without the assistance of humans. When that happens, it is most often the other way around: the white bass is the mama and the striped bass, the papa.

But the average angler who catches a Bodie Bass, whether on natural or artificial bait, could care less about the genetics of the fish. The angler is too busy admiring the fish.

Although the Bodie Bass can be caught on artificial lures about any time of the year, Bob Bailey of Rockingham County prefers to use natural bait—especially live shad in the spring and summer. He generally uses artificial lures only in the fall.

And Bob knows as much about the Bodie Bass as any angler. He is a weekend fishing guide who specializes in this hybrid and has made a study of its habits. Although none of his clients has ever tried to fish for it with a fly rod, the fly rod angler who wants to catch one could learn much from Bob.

When using artificial lures, Bob favors such topwater offerings as Zara Spooks. When he goes under the water, he likes Redfins, large Hot Spots and other such lures. In other words, about the same things that you would use for striped bass. So about any fly that would appeal to a striped bass should appeal to the Bodie Bass.

Stanley Winbourne, a very good all-around fly fisherman, has caught most of his Bodie Bass on Clousers Minnows. That should be no surprise because the Clouser is high on the list of many of North Carolina's best fly rodders as a good fly to use for most fish under most circumstances.

The hybrid bass, which is known by different names in different states, has now been stocked in a number of lakes, usually smaller ones, around North Carolina. For up-to-date information on where you may now catch them, contact the North Carolina Wildlife Resources Commission in Raleigh.

Incidentally, you may want to release those Bodie Bass that you believe can survive. Being a hybrid, it can reproduce only rarely. So the ones you don't release must be replaced by stocking.

Photo by Buck Paysour

Some good flies for crappie. Top row, left to right: Charlie's bonefish fly;no-name fly tied by author to resemble crappie jig; fly tied by Marshall Coble. Bottom row: Clouser Minnow tied by John Baskervill, left; spinner fly, right. These flies will catch other fish as well.

Chapter Twelve

Crappie: Fun and Delicious

...a rose by any other name would smell as sweet.

Shakespeare probably had never heard of a fish called the "crappie" when he wrote that line. But if he had, he might have written that a crappie by any other name would taste as sweet and be just as much fun to catch—especially on a fly rod.

You can, of course, use about any kind of fishing equipment to catch crappie, which are called speckled perch in some areas and mispronounced "croppie" in others. But as with other species, it is more sporting to use a fly rod. Even though crappie are not known as good fighters, they put up an acceptable tussle on a light trout rod—say a rod that weighs two ounces or so.

A friend, Marshall Coble, likes to fish for crappie with a light eight-and-a-half-foot rod (matched for a five-weight line).

"That rod gives me a little more distance than a shorter rod, but it is still light enough so that it doesn't take away the fun as much as a heavier rod would," he says.

Sometimes, if there is not too much wind, Marshall switches to a light nine-foot rod matched for a four-weight line. But most of the time, he uses the shorter and slightly heavier rod because when there is a breeze, he tries to fish

153

the windy side of the lake. As do many other species of fish, crappie like to take advantage of the wind, lying where food will be blown their way. Then you need the heavier rod to throw your fly into the teeth of the wind and into the teeth of the fish.

Marshall, who guides for smallmouth bass anglers on weekends (see Chapter Six), ties a fly especially for crappie fishing. It is white (see photo) and has rubber legs.

Usually, Marshall ties the fly without any weight. Sometimes he will add a small amount of weight, say one turn of lead wire, to make the fly sink a little faster and a little deeper.

When he needs to fish much deeper for crappie, he uses weighted flies such as the Sheep Fly, or a small Clouser.

Some people use a Charlie, a bonefish fly, for crappie. Other favorite flies for fishing a little deeper than Marshall's unweighted flies include Zonkers, weighted Woolly Worms and Woolly Buggers. I tie a fly that looks much like a crappie jig (see photo), a lure that is usually cast on an ultralight spinning rod. I wrap a couple of turns of lead wire on a Six or Eight hook, tie some marabou at the rear of the hook and make a body of chenille.

Often, it makes little difference what you use for crappie. They are not finicky and on some days will hit about any fly or streamer that will get down to the proper depth. Believe it or not, I have caught crappie on plain gold hooks. This happened several times when I ran out of bait while fishing with live minnows. But this is unusual. Usually, you need a fly or other artificial lure or natural bait to catch crappie.

A small spinner fly, a combination of an "in-line" spinner and a fly, is another good thing to use for crappie. Sometimes a spinner with a plain hook will take them. Another trick is to add a tiny piece of pork rind or other small attractor to the hook. Using pork rind is the closest I will come to using natural bait on a fly rod. I am not snobbish in my fishing and don't mind using natural bait when I fish with spinning or casting equipment or with cane poles. Nor do I recoil at the thought of somebody else using natural bait such as minnows or earthworms or crickets on a fly rod. But I don't ever use natural bait on a fly rod. That is not my idea of fly fishing.

As a general rule, Marshall Coble likes Size Six flies. His favorite colors include white, gray and shad. Crappie love small shad. Marshall also likes flies that have chartreuse bodies and heads that are black. But no matter what the dominant color fly or streamer Marshall ties for crappie, he usually adds a touch of red to it.

He has caught crappie on flies as early as January. Normally, however, he starts fly fishing for them in late February and continues on through about mid-May—depending, of course, on the weather. He begins fly fishing for crappie again in the early fall, when the water starts to cool. He continues fishing for them on through about mid-November—again depending on the weather.

Marshall fishes for crappie with a fly rod about the same way you fish for them with live bait or lures such as jigs. He fishes around brush piles, willow bushes, boat docks, and other cover. Many die-hard crappie anglers gather Christmas trees at the end of the Yule season and sink them in the crappie waters to create cover. If you know where any of these have been submerged, you often can catch crappie. Sometimes you will also catch bass and bream and other fish on the same flies that you use for crappie.

Among the good qualities of crappie is that they are often easy to catch, especially when they are in shallow or moderately deep water. They usually travel or congregate in schools and, where you catch one, you can often catch dozens of others without even moving.

Another good thing about crappie is that they are widely distributed throughout North Carolina and much of the rest of the country. They are found in much of North Carolina's fresh and brackish waters, including many municipal water supply lakes.

North Carolina has both kinds of crappie: the black crappie and white crappie. The difference between the two species is really academic when it comes to the fun they provide. They are equally delicious.

Marshall Coble catches many of his crappie in farm ponds. When fishing farm ponds, he usually fishes from the bank. Occasionally, he will wade or use a canoe or a float tube (see Chapter Sixteen). He also does well in Falls of the Neuse Lake, Lake Badin, Lake Farmer, Lake Jordan, Lake Thom-A-Lex, and the Uwharrie River.

Kerr Lake (Buggs Island) on the North Carolina-Virginia border is an excellent place to catch crappie. So is the Alligator River, an Eastern North Carolina brackish-water stream. Unless there is a lot of wind, the Alligator is an especially easy place to catch crappie because the river is relatively shallow. Many other Eastern North Carolina rivers and creeks hold crappie.

Crappie are so prolific that there are no legal size or creel limits on most North Carolina waters. There are a few exceptions, however. If you are not sure, you should check the regulations for the areas you plan to fish.

Some people use sinking or sink-tip fly lines to fish for crappie. But Marshall Coble and most other anglers I know just about always use floating lines. It is great fun to see the line twitch, then spurt across the water, signaling a strike.

If there is a little wrinkle on the water, that will often give Marshall's fly about all the action it needs to attract crappie. If the water is smooth, Marshall will twitch his fly or make it dart by stripping in line. There is hardly any wrong way of working a fly for crappie.

The biggest secret to catching crappie is finding the depth at which they are feeding at the time you are fishing. Once you learn that, crappie will usually—but not always—hit at that same depth.

"Even if I have caught fish at a certain depth, I will fish deeper if the fish I have been catching are small," Marshall says.

He believes many schools consist of crappie of similar sizes.

When crappie are not holding too deep and you are using a floating line, you can adjust the depth of your fly by lengthening or shortening your leader. Or, if you are using a heavy fly and a small-diameter floating line, you can use a fly that has enough weight to sink the first few feet of the front of your line.

Although I have caught a few crappie on a floating fly or popper when I was fishing for bass and bream, those incidents were flukes. You almost always catch crappie under the water, but they will occasionally hit just a few inches under the water at the right time and in the right water.

I once worried that I was destined never to be a good crappie fly rod angler.

Sure, beginning when I was just a little boy hardly old enough to hold a cane pole and continuing through adulthood, I caught countless crappie. I caught them on cane poles. I caught them on casting rods. I caught them on spinning rods. I caught them on natural bait. I caught them on artificial lures. The crappie has long been one of my favorite fishes. And fly fishing, since I took it up some years earlier, has been my favorite method of fishing. I caught, on my fly rod, many other fish that were supposed to be more difficult to catch on flies.

Yet the only crappie I had ever managed to catch on a fly rod were caught by accident. I could never catch crappie with a fly rod when I was trying to catch crappie.

It was frustrating, especially since my fly fishing buddies kept telling me about how easy it was to catch crappie on flies. My chagrin was compounded by the fact that I knew my friends were telling the truth. Crappie are among the least sophisticated of fishes. They will almost jump into your boat, especially in the spring and fall.

I remember fishing the Alligator River with John Peterson, Claibourne Darden and Curtis Youngblood when crappie almost did jump into the boat that Curtis and I were fishing in. All I had to do was drop a small jig a few inches below the boat, and a crappie would grab it.

I could have put a jig on a fly rod and caught them then, I know. But that, to my mind, would be like fishing natural bait on a fly rod. It just would not have been fly fishing.

Goodness knows, over the years I had tried hard enough to catch these simple fish on a fly rod. I fished the fly rod in places where I had caught plenty of crappie on other types of tackle. I fished the fly rod for crappie at the same times of the year when I had always caught crappie on other types of tackle. I fished for crappie with flies that my friends had suggested.

You may not believe what I am about to tell you. But, so help me, it is the truth. Often, after I had caught crappie after crappie on spinning tackle, I would pick up my fly rod and cast a streamer or other sinking fly into the same spot where I had just caught crappie. But not one single lowly crappie would take my fly.

Then, after much failure, an idea hit me. Why not ask Greg Campbell for help?

Greg puts most of his own angling efforts into fishing for largemouth bass with spinning and baitcasting gear and is very good with both. He does not use a fly rod, however, and he rarely fishes for crappie.

Still he has studied the habits of many species of fish, including the crappie, and I was sure he would know where I would stand a chance of catching crappie on a fly rod. Or at the least, I thought, he would know somebody who knew where I might catch crappie on a fly rod.

So I called Greg and, like a patient seeking advice from a psychiatrist, told him my problem.

"I'm not much of a crappie fisherman," Greg said. "But I'll talk to Jeff Heath. He caught a lot of crappie last week."

A few days later, Greg called back.

"Can you go fishing at 4:30 on Monday afternoon?" he asked.

At the appointed time, I met Greg at a local lake. He launched his boat and I hopped in.

It was a muggy summer afternoon, not the best time for crappie fishing, especially crappie fishing with a fly rod. Still, I had decided that I would catch crappie on flies or not catch them at all on this day. I had even left my spinning gear at home.

"There is a line of submerged Christmas trees along here," Greg said after using his electric trolling motor to position his boat off a point. "This is where Jeff caught his crappie."

Then Greg, despite his claim that he was not a good crappie fisherman, quickly caught a couple on his spinning rod

159

and a small jig. Using a two-ounce, seven-foot rod, I whipped a small Zonker a couple dozen times in the heavy and sultry air. After each cast, I let the Zonker sink to the depth at which Greg was catching his crappie. Then I began the retrieve. Nothing happened. Would this trip end in disappointment as had so many others?

But then I felt a tug, followed by the pull of a hooked fish. I stripped in line and landed the first crappie I had ever intentionally caught on a fly rod. Greg landed a couple more, yet I couldn't get another hit on the Zonker. So I switched to a small Clouser Minnow that John Baskervill had tied. On the third cast, I caught a crappie.

After a couple more casts, my fly rod quivered again. Thinking I had a bite from another crappie, I gently set the hook. (Crappie have delicate mouths and you will pull the hook out if you are too aggressive.) My fish immediately made a lunge, informing me that it was something much larger and more powerful than a crappie.

The fish stayed far below the surface, swimming stubbornly for a long time, leading Greg and me to speculate that it was a large catfish.

"I don't care what it is," I said. "It's fun."

My four-pound leader briefly snagged on the Christmas trees, making me fear I was going to lose my Clouser Minnow and my fish. Luckily, the leader freed itself before the fish could break off.

Greg maneuvered the boat to help me keep the leader away from the electric and gasoline motor propellers as I continued to work the fish.

"I wonder if it could be a carp," I told Greg.

Finally, I coaxed the fish up out of the depths, and we saw it for the first time.

"It's a bass," Greg announced.

We didn't have a landing net, but Greg deftly grabbed the fish by its bottom jaw and hoisted it in the boat.

The largemouth bass weighed only three pounds and eleven ounces, but considering that I had caught it on such a light rod and a light leader, I was as proud of it as if it had weighed twice as much. Although it was not even close to the largest bass I had ever caught on a fly rod, it was one of the largest I had ever caught on such a light fly rod. We released it.

The irony of what had just happened did not escape me. The only times in the past when I had caught crappie on a fly rod had been when I was fishing for bass or some other species. Now I had caught a bass when I was fishing for crappie.

In the meantime, Jeff Heath rowed his boat out to join us.

"That was a nice fish you just caught," he said.

I beamed.

Jeff soon proved he was a good fisherman. Using a spinning rod and a small jig, he caught crappie on almost every cast.

Greg caught plenty of crappie too.

I caught a number of crappie on my fly rod, though not nearly as many as Greg and Jeff caught.

I caught enough that I decided to experiment to see what flies I could catch them on. I caught them on Clousers, Zonkers, Charlie's Bonefish flies and several no-name flies I had tied myself. We all also caught some nice bream.

I didn't mind that Greg and Jeff outfished me. I rationalized that one of my fish, on the featherweight rod, gave me as much fun as several of theirs gave them.

161

Besides, I had broken my jinx as a crappie fly fisherman. I was confident that I would catch more on fly rods in the future.

And I have.

Chapter Thirteen

White Bass and White Perch

Remember those flies that you used to catch crappie? Take care of them. One day, you may need them when you find yourself surrounded by fish that are whipping the water to froth, slashing minnows.

Some of the minnows, attempting to escape death, are leaping out of the water in tiny showers of sparkling spray. You quickly make a false cast and shoot your small white Zonker into the center of the melee. The streamer barely brushes the water before something belts it.

The result, you know from past experience, would have been the same no matter what fly you had cast. It could have been a cork popper, a Woolly Bugger, a Woolly Worm, a deer hair bug, or about anything else in your fly box. You could even have cast a cigarette butt, a pencil stub, a stick of chewing gum and one of the marauding fish would have jumped on it.

Are you surrounded by gorging bluefish? No. You are fishing in fresh water, and the fish are much smaller than the typical bluefish. But it is hard to imagine even a bluefish giving you more excitement, ounce for ounce, especially because you caught this fish on an ultralight trout rod whereas you would have to use a much heavier rod for bluefish.

The fish thrashing the water around your boat are white bass.

Today, you are fishing Lake Tillery. But you could have been fishing in any other of the Yadkin River chain of lakes, or in Fontana Lake, Kerr Lake, Lake Jordan, Lake Norman, or a dozen or more other North Carolina lakes in which white bass have been stocked.

True, white bass are smaller than some other fish. They live a maximum of about four years. So they don't have time to get to be very big. A two-pounder is rare and a four-pounder is considered trophy size. But few other fish provide the thrill that white bass will give you—especially when they are schooling on top. Then they are easy to find and easy to catch. They will whack your fly with vicious abandon.

To locate surface-feeding white bass, you need only to cruise a lake until you spot a school or schools churning the water. Or sometimes you can find them by watching for flocks of gulls. Like bluefish, white bass often seem to kill their prey just for the sheer pleasure of killing. They leave many of their victims dead or dying on the water, and gulls congregate to feed on the remains. Some white bass anglers carry binoculars to help them spot schools of fish or flocks of gulls.

After locating a school, you cut your gasoline motor before you get too close and use your trolling motor to ease within casting range of the fish. Then, you are likely to get a strike on every cast at least for several minutes. After you catch some fish from a school, the school will usually sink from sight. When this happens, you again scan the water around you; frequently, the school will surface again not far away. You once again ease close enough to cast to the school and catch more fish.

Sometimes, when white bass are schooling on top, more than one school will surface close enough for you to be able to cast to them with your fly rod. When that happens, you can cast to one school while your partner casts to another. As a rule, catching fish from a school does not seem to spook the others. They apparently move only when the minnows they are chasing move.

White bass usually school on top in the fall more often than any other time of the year. But they can feed on top in the spring and sometimes even on the hottest summer days. Then they customarily school late in the day.

But occasionally they will school all day even on a scorching day. A friend, Jack Bilyeu, and I caught white bass on top on Lake Tillery on a cloudless summer day when temperatures hovered near one hundred degrees. The fish schooled all day, and we fished even through noon, gulping Gatorade and cold water to keep from becoming dehydrated. I kept dipping my cap in the lake to provide my skin a little relief. The white bass I caught that day years ago were the first I had ever caught. Since then, they have been one of my favorite species.

Many fly rod anglers think that the most thrilling way to catch surface-schooling white bass is with small-to-medium-size poppers or other surface lures. But other good anglers argue that you'll catch more, and often bigger, white bass by using streamers or other underwater flies—even when the fish are schooling on top. When you use sinking flies, they say, you'll not only catch fish that are feeding on top but also fish that are lurking under the surface school. Often the larger fish will swim under the surface-feeding school, waiting for the easy pickings to fall down to them.

As for whether topwater or underwater flies give you the most thrill, it often doesn't make much difference when white bass are schooling on top. The fish wallop your sinking fly as soon as it kisses the water, so it is just like topwater fishing anyway.

When you fish to surface schools of white bass, you should be aware that striped bass will often swim under the white bass. If you expect this, you might want to use a heavier fly rod. It will take away some of the fight of the white bass but will have the backbone to help you land the much larger striped bass.

You can catch white bass on a fly rod even when they are below the surface. You just need to find them, which is a little more difficult to do than when they are schooling on top.

You can use a depth finder to locate them. Or you can use the old-fashion way to find them: troll for them with baitcasting or spinning equipment until you start catching them, then switch to your fly rod.

One way to do this is to use a tandem rig behind a deep-running plug such as a Bomber. You first tie a tiny spoon like a shad spoon—about any tiny spoon will do—approximately thirty-six inches behind the deep-running lure. Next, you use a dropper loop to attach a small crappie jig or shad dart about halfway between the spoon and the diving lure.

The diving lure provides action to the jig and spoon and gets them down to where the white bass are cruising. Most of the time, white bass will hit the jig or spoon but they will occasionally hit the plug. I have even caught a few striped bass while I was trolling for white bass in Lake Tillery. That's why it's a good idea to use fairly heavy line, say fifteen- to twenty-pound test, for your running line and lighter line—ten-pound test is a good choice—for the tandem rig. That way, you have strong enough line to land the striper that might hit your plug but when you hang up the small spoon or crappie jig and have to break off the tandem rig, you don't lose your plug.

Some good white bass trollers, such as Cliff and Latta Fitzgerald of High Rock Lake, use sinkers that weigh three-quarters of an ounce or more, instead of plugs, to get their white bass lures down to the fish.

No matter which rig you use, once you catch one or more white bass while trolling, you go back and troll the same area again. Where you catch one white bass, you usually catch others. Most of the time, they travel in packs even when they are feeding under the water.

Consequently, after catching fish on several trolling passes, you can cut off your gasoline motor, use your electric motor to ease within casting distance of where the fish are, pick up your fly rod, and use a Clouser Minnow or other weighted streamers to fish.

(Some anglers who troll for white bass use their electric motors instead of their gasoline motors. Others believe it makes little difference, and prefer to use their gasoline motors and conserve battery power in the event they need to use the electric motor for some other purpose before the end of the day.)

White bass that are schooling below the surface generally will hit any medium-size streamer when they are schooling on top. A light-colored streamer is usually the best color because it is about the same color as shad minnows, a favorite quarry of white bass. Some white bass anglers prefer something with a little flash in it. But it bears repeating: when white bass are really foraging, it usually doesn't make much difference what you use as long as it isn't too big.

One of the best times to catch white bass on sinking flies is in the spring while the fish are on their spawning runs. Then they run up into creeks and rivers from lakes where they spend most of the rest of the year.

Vince Davis, a Forsyth County fly fisherman, fishes several stretches of the Yadkin River from his canoe during those times.

He prefers to use rods matched for four-weight to six-weight lines for the white bass. Since catching his first ones by accident he has caught a hundred or more in a day. He uses a small sinking fly that imitates shad.

Apparently, white bass are just as voracious when they make their spawning run as they are when they are schooling on top in lakes.

"Minnows were spilling out of the mouths of some of those that I caught," Vince says.

While fishing for white bass, he has also caught striped bass below Tuckertown Lake. In fact, he caught the first striped bass he ever caught on a fly rod during a float trip while fishing for white bass.

White Perch

Speaking of shad-colored streamers, you can use them and most of the other flies that you used on crappie and white bass to catch another of my favorite fishes: the white perch.

The white perch and the white bass have similar habits. That is understandable. Both are members of the *Percichthyidae* family. They even look a little alike. But the white perch has only one distinct stripe down each side of its body whereas the white bass has about ten dark lines on each the side.

Yet, although the cousins sometimes live together in North Carolina, some waters contain only one of the two species.

Photo by Buck Paysour

This white bass, caught on Lake Thom-A-Lex in Davidson County, hit a Jig-A-Bugger, which is also a good fly for white perch.

In North Carolina, for example, white bass—as far I have been able to determine—are not found in the brackish waters of Eastern North Carolina. Both species, however, sometimes inhabit the same waters in inland North Carolina. This is true, for example, of Yadkin and Pee Dee River lakes such as High Rock Lake, Lake Tillery, and Blewett Falls.

But in other North Carolina waters, especially those of Eastern North Carolina, only white perch are plentiful.

The white perch is adaptable. It can live in salt water, fresh water, and brackish water. That's not true of the white bass. It is essentially a freshwater fish.

The white perch and white bass will, however, take the same flies and other lures—with some exceptions.

One thing they have in common is that they each run in schools and are often easy to catch. Where you catch one, you are likely to catch others. Yet, seldom do you see white perch schooling on top of the water with the rapaciousness that white bass often display. White perch are more likely to just dimple the water when they do feed on top. The disturbance they make on the surface is usually more like that made by raindrops in a light shower. Surface-feeding white perch are often after insects whereas surface-schooling white bass are almost always after minnows of some kind.

For that reason, you seldom catch white perch on fly rod poppers whereas white bass will, when they are schooling, hit poppers with a vengeance. On the other hand, white perch that are dimpling the water will sometimes take dry flies, things that are almost too dainty to appeal to white bass.

When white perch are below the surface, they will take the same flies and streamers that appeal to white bass: small and medium-size Zonkers, Clousers, Woolly Worms, Woolly

Buggers, and so on. White or predominantly white streamers, particularly those with a little flash or glitter, are good for white perch, just as they are for white bass or crappie. White bass, when they are schooling on the surface, will generally clobber a streamer before it has time to settle whereas surface schooling white perch prefer to wait until it drops.

Yet white perch, when hooked on a light fly rod, show much of the same gusto that white bass show.

My favorite place to fish for white perch is in the brackish waters or sheltered salt waters of Eastern North Carolina. For one thing, those that are caught there are better to eat than those that come from inland lakes. Saltwater and brackish-water white perch are, in my opinion, among the most delicious of fishes. They are easy to filet and are good to eat no matter how you cook them. I release most fish I catch, but white perch are among the exceptions. They are so prolific that sports anglers could hardly put a dent in their populations.

Some people label white perch "Waccamaw Perch" no matter where they catch them because Lake Waccamaw in southeastern North Carolina is a famous place to fish for them. At Lake Waccamaw and in some other Eastern North Carolina waters, some fishermen "call" the fish by whipping poles on the water. The theory is that this sounds like feeding fish and attracts the white perch.

The strange thing about this is that, as mentioned earlier, white perch rarely school noisily and energetically on top. But the tactic must work for anglers. Otherwise, they wouldn't do it. Perhaps the white perch think that the noise comes from other species of schooling fish, and the white perch come to get the table scraps. This makes sense because white perch often school along with striped bass, especially in Eastern North Carolina.

171

Usually when you catch one perch at a certain depth, you'll find that others are at about that same depth, at least for a while.

"The main thing is to find the perch," Booty Spruill, a former Currituck Sound guide, said.

Another one of the many things that I like about the white perch, especially the Eastern North Carolina variety, is its willingness to hit shallow-running streamers even in the hottest days of summer. Some people even think they hit better in hot weather than during other times of the year. They start getting really active in the spring and continue through the fall.

Where there are crappie, white perch and white bass in the same water, you'll often catch all three species, because they all like some of the same foods and will hit some of the same artificial lures.

Chapter Fourteen

Mixed Bag on a Fly Rod

John Baskervill is fishing Scranton Creek, an Eastern North Carolina stream where he has often caught large-mouth bass. John, as do many other good anglers, thinks that underwater streamers will catch more fish day in and day out than will poppers or other surface fly rod lures. Still, he enjoys the commotion that fish make when they charge a topwater enticement. So he has decided to start out using a bass bug on this morning.

He flips the bug to the mouth of a small feeder creek, lets it sit briefly, and then begins popping it.

KA-BLOOM!

John's eight-and-half-foot rod bows, and John wrestles a fish to the boat.

It is not a largemouth bass. It is a puppy drum, a saltwater fish. This is not an unusual occurrence. John often catches puppy drum and some other saltwater fish, along with largemouth bass and some other freshwater fish, on a popper in this kind of water.

"When you can find puppy drum in shallow water, they will often blast a popper," he says.

But, to repeat, John usually fishes streamers or other underwater flies—especially when he is fishing water that holds both saltwater fish and freshwater fish.

Catching different kinds of fish—both freshwater and saltwater—on top or under the water is a big part of the allure of fishing streams such as Scranton Creek. The creek, as are many others in Eastern North Carolina, is usually brackish. That means it is salty enough to hold many species of saltwater fish but not too salty for many varieties of freshwater fish.

Consequently, you never know, when you cast your fly upon brackish waters, what kind of fish you will catch next. Striped bass often swim with largemouth bass; pumpkin-seed with puppy drum, chain pickerel with redfin pickerel; white perch with yellow perch; bluefish with bluegill bream; crappie with croaker; and sea trout with summer flounder.

John Baskervill has caught them all—and other species, too—while fishing this kind of water with a fly rod.

It is called "mixed-bag fishing"—my favorite kind of fishing.

You can often experience this sort of fly fishing in tributaries that feed into all of North Carolina's sounds and into the ocean itself. The quality of fishing in many of these waters often varies, however, from year to year. In some years, it will be sensational on a particular stream and poor on other streams. Then it will change and, for several years, will be so poor that you think that pollution, or the invasion of too much salt water, or something else has ruined the fishing. Then the fishing becomes good again.

Take Scranton Creek, where John Baskervill caught that puppy drum on a popping bug. I fished the creek for years, almost always catching fish. At various times, I caught white perch, yellow perch, several varieties of bream and other small sunfish, an occasional sea trout, a few bluefish, many chain pickerel, a fair number of largemouth bass, and others.

Scranton Creek, on a beautiful fall day, rewarded me with one of the biggest largemouth bass that I have ever caught on a fly rod—though not even close to the biggest I have caught on any type of tackle. My partner on the trip, John Ellison, and I landed a variety of fish, including white perch, yellow perch, bream, and largemouth bass. Also, a couple of striped bass hit John's lure. They hit short, however, something unusual for stripers in that water. Most of the time, they hit so hard that they hook themselves. There was no doubt that the fish that hit John's lures were stripers; the water was so clear that we could see them. Perhaps they, too, could see so well that they weren't sure that the lure was something they really wanted to sink their teeth into.

John and I fished to the mouth of the creek, which flows into a wide section of the Pungo River. In the exposed opening, heavy waves sloshed against the boat and the marsh, and I had difficulty holding the boat steady enough for us to fish. Nevertheless John and I both managed to make some decent casts with our fly rods. I dropped my homemade black bass bug against the marsh. Almost as soon as the bug hit the water, something smashed it, and a big bass hurdled from the water.

I had trouble maintaining a tight line because the boat kept washing toward the marsh. My fly line ended up around my neck like a hangman's noose. Then my bass sought cover deep in the marsh.

"I'm going to lose my fish," I moaned. "I'm going to lose him."

"Take it easy," John said, holding the landing net.

At last, I managed to back the boat from the marsh while holding my rod high to keep the line away from the prop of the electric motor. I tapped on the rod grip, which sent vibrations down the line, causing the fish to scoot out of the reeds. John hoisted the bass up with the landing net.

On the way back to the motel, we stopped at a country store to weigh the bass, which lacked a few ounces of being seven pounds. It created a stir among the hangers-on at the store because bass, though sometimes plentiful, do not commonly grow to be as big in those waters as they do in some inland waters.

I recall other good fishing trips to Scranton Creek, especially one Doris Dale and I made, also on a fall day. We had fished Pungo Creek the day before under a balmy sun, not catching a single fish, not even getting a strike. During the night, rain began to fall and temperatures dropped.

The next day, we towed our boat to Scranton Creek. Like Pungo Creek, Scranton is a tributary to the Pungo River. The Pungo, in turn, flows into the Pamlico River, which feeds into Pamlico Sound.

Before launching our boat at Scranton Creek, Doris Dale and I donned our foul weather suits for protection against the chilly rain.

We caught fish after fish. Almost every cast I made with my fly rod produced a largemouth. Doris Dale, using closed-face spinning gear and a black Jitterbug, caught a number of largemouth. When she switched to an underwater Rebel-type lure, she caught several striped bass.

Temperatures continued to plunge, and, at about 11 A.M., Doris Dale turned toward me.

"Tell me," she said, "are we having fun yet?"

Her lips were blue, and she was shivering from the cold.

"Reel in your line, Honey," I replied. "We're going home."

It was about noon when we pulled the boat out of the water. There's no telling how many fish we could have caught if we had kept fishing.

Soon after that, something happened to the fishing in Scranton Creek. I fished it a dozen or so times in the next several years, catching only a few fish. So I abandoned the creek for other waters.

Then my son, Conrad, moved to Belhaven on the Pungo River to practice law. He decided to move there, by the way, partly because he and I often visited the town to fish when he was a little boy. Anyway, one day after Conrad had settled down in Belhaven, my older son, John, and I visited him and his wife, Jan, one late April weekend. Conrad had to work, and John and I decided to fish. I suggested we try Scranton Creek, thinking that if we did not catch anything in a couple of hours, we could pull our boat out of the water and go somewhere else.

We did not have to move. We caught plenty of fish, including a good-size largemouth bass I caught on my fly rod and even a bigger one that John caught on a spinning rod.

I caught several other species of fish, including the largest pumpkinseed I had ever seen—all on my fly rod. I also hooked a large chain pickerel (jack), also on my fly rod. The jack swirled and threw the streamer. The next morning, John and I went back to Scranton Creek and caught more fish.

In some years, you can catch a variety of freshwater and saltwater fish on a fly rod in just about any Eastern North Carolina brackish water.

Most streams that flow directly or indirectly into the Pamlico or Albemarle sounds are good places to try mixed bag fly fishing. You can fish many stretches of these streams in a modest-size boat. Some of these waters include the Alligator River, Big Flatty and Little Flatty Creeks, Little River, Neuse River, North River, Pamlico River, Pungo River, Roanoke River, and others. The tributaries of those rivers and creeks also often hold many varieties of fish. So do the sheltered bays and coves of the sounds themselves.

Or if you would like to try pure saltwater fly fishing in a relatively small boat and relatively light fly gear, sheltered areas of other parts of the Outer Banks are great places for that. So are sheltered areas in the lower reaches of rivers such as the White Oak and Cape Fear.

Most good fly fishermen I know say they would choose the Clouser Minnow if they were restricted to one fly for mixed-bag fishing in any kind of water—salt, fresh or brackish. The Clouser Minnow is, in effect, a fly rod jig, and you know how deadly a jig can be no matter what kind of equipment it is fished on.

I have caught more fish in North Carolina brackish water on Zonkers than any other streamer. I guess that's because I was using the Zonker when I caught the first fish I ever caught on a streamer and now continue to use it more than other streamers. You'll usually catch more fish on a streamer or other fly that you have faith in. It's the same principle as hunting. If you have confidence in your hunting dog, you're going to do better than hunting with a dog that you don't have confidence in.

Even though Zonkers are not usually tied weedless, you can buy them from L. L. Bean (see Appendix B) with hooks that ride up or tie them that way yourself. Turned-up hooks enable Zonkers to come through weeds, usually with the greatest of ease. Zonkers look more like minnows than most streamers. They are relatively light and cast well but also sink slowly but deep. Often, you'll get a strike if you pause and let the Zonker flutter downward when it reaches a clear spot in the grass.

Much of Eastern North Carolina's brackish water is weedy, incidentally, so you will do better to fish semi-weedless streamers and poppers there. There is no such thing as

Photo by John Paysour

Author caught this largemouth bass on a Zonker streamer in brackish water of Scranton Creek.

A Zonker, the author's favorite streamer fly.

Photo by Buck Paysour

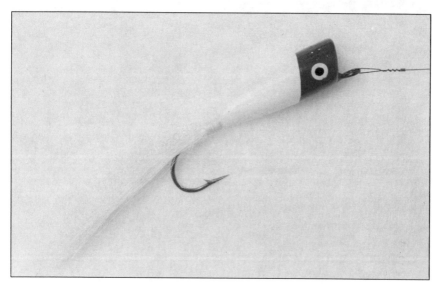

Photo by Leger Meyland

Bluefish popper favored by Stanley Winbourne. Wire attached to eye of hook prevents fish from biting through leader. Stripers and other saltwater fish also will hit this lure.

a completely weedless fly, of course. If there were, it would also be fishless. A fish couldn't get to the hook. Although you don't seem to lose many fish on streamers whose hooks are upturned, bass bugs whose hooks are upturned seem less effective in hooking fish. So you may want to consider using loops of monofilament or something else (see Chapter Three) to make your bugs semi-weedless.

Almost any cork popper is good for mixed bag fishing. Hair bugs, especially the Dahlberg's Diver, is potent on many days. But, as John Baskervill says, you'll catch more different kinds of fish on streamers than you will on floating bugs.

Some good streamers to use for mixed-bag fishing in Eastern North Carolina (in addition to the Zonker) include the Bendback, the Deceiver, the Woolly Bugger, and the spinner fly. These, in medium sizes, will catch just about any fish that swims in brackish water. A medium-size spinner fly is good for all-around fishing. The Woolly Worm or G. Neil fly or any other nymph will sometimes catch about all the bream and other small sunfish you care to catch in brackish water. So will a small spinner fly. Most of the year, small poppers are also deadly for bream and other small sunfish.

The "Jig-A-Bugger," a small and flashy weighted fly, is good to use for white perch (see Chapter Thirteen) and other small brackish-water fish. White is usually the best color for perch. I order my Jig-A-Buggers from Kaufmann's Streamborn Inc. (see Appendix B). Other sinking flies that are white will also take perch and other brackish-water panfish. Size Six seems to be a good choice.

Spinner flies fished slowly on the bottom will even take flounder. Often, it doesn't make much difference what size you use; big flounder will sometimes take small spinners and small flounder will sometimes take large spinners in North Carolina brackish water.

Sometimes, small and medium-size bluefish will invade North Carolina brackish-water streams. About any medium-size or large streamer or popper will take bluefish. It's a good idea to use a few inches of wire leader on your popper (see photo) or streamer if you expect to catch large bluefish. A large bluefish's teeth will slash monofilament line. If you are fishing for snapper (little) bluefish with a relatively small popper, however, you may also want to use heavy monofilament instead of wire for a shock leader. Wire could sink a small popper.

A big jack can also bite through your leader, though not as readily as does a big bluefish. Some fly rod anglers use a few inches of heavy monofilament line between their flies and the tippets of their leaders when they expect to catch jack. Jack, incidentally, are about as much fun to catch on a fly rod as any fish that swims. They are especially exciting when they attack a popping bug. They tear up the water and, once hooked, fight hard, jumping and tail walking time after time. They are long, streamlined fish, built like their relatives, the northern pike and muskellunge, and have nasty dispositions to match. Jack also have another appealing quality: they will hit streamers just about all year including in the dead of winter.

Although John Baskervill enjoys catching species such as puppy drum and other brackish-water or saltwater fish on a fly rod, he often starts out using spinning gear. Then, when he catches fish, he switches to the fly rod.

"You need to find them first," he explains.

One good way to find fish is to try what I call the "Dave Goforth Method," a method that involves using small jigs trimmed with soft plastic or other dressing and sweetened with small strips of fish. Dave, who was an expert at this kind of fishing, cut the strips thin so that they would swing or flutter—almost like pork rind strips. He crawled the lure across the bottom of the water, raising and lowering his rod, similar to the way many people fish artificial worms.

Dave fished the lure with ultralight equipment and light line, most often two-pound test. On occasion, he would fish four-pound test and on a rare occasion, he would step up to six-pound. Amazingly, he rarely lost even a big fish on the light line. He knew how to play fish and take advantage of the spring in his rod and other characteristics of his equipment.

Dave began developing this method of fishing after his buddy, Sam Snead, had to leave Currituck Sound early to play in a golf tournament. Dave stayed behind to fish by himself for a while.

"I fished along some marsh where Sam and I had caught only a few fish," Dave recalled later. "I said to myself, 'There should be more fish along that bank.'"

So Dave started experimenting. He made a small lure more savory by adding a strip of cut fish to it and soon began to catch fish after fish of several varieties. Over the years, he refined this into the most deadly method of fishing I have ever used.

After you use Dave's method to find fish, you can pick up your fly rod and, hopefully, catch fish with it.

Incidentally, one good way to catch your "sweetener" is to use a fly rod and a small nymph such as a Woolly Worm or a bream popper. You can almost always catch a small sunfish on one of these. Then you use strips (see photo) of the sunfish on a jig or other small lure on spinning gear to catch larger fish. After you catch several larger fish (finding them, as John Baskervill suggests) you switch back to a fly rod, only a heavier one this time, to catch a mixed bag of fish.

183

Photo by Buck Paysour

This typical Dave Goforth rig uses natural bait for finding fish in brackish water.

Although Dave's method is effective about anywhere, it is especially good for brackish water because it will catch just about any species of fish. And brackish water often holds an astonishing variety of fish.

I caught the first saltwater fish that I caught on a fly rod by following John Baskervill's admonition to "find them first" and employing Dave Goforth's method to find them.

Ron Miller, book editor and editorial writer for the Greensboro *News & Record*, and I were fishing together on tributaries to the Pamlico Sound. My two sons, John and Conrad, were fishing nearby in John's boat. The other two members of our party, Curtis Youngblood and Emmett Sumner, fished in Emmett's boat.

Ron and I had fished an hour or so during which I used my fly rod with little success. Ron, using a spinning rod, had caught only a few sand perch, a species that I could not identify at the time. I picked up my spinning rod and also caught a couple.

Finally, I said, "Why don't we try the Dave Goforth Method?"

I picked up my seven-foot mountain-trout rod, tied a bream popper on the end of the four-pound test leader, and made a couple of casts to the marsh.

In just a few minutes, a nice pumpkinseed bream took the popper.

I quickly killed it, sliced some small strips from its side, and gave Ron one, which he impaled on a small jig head. I put a strip of the fish on some jigs I had fashioned myself especially for Dave's method.

In a minute or two, Ron leaned back.

"I've got one," he said.

He reeled in a fish about twelve inches long that put up a commendable struggle on the light action rod.

"What is it?" he asked, holding it by the line.

It was a bluefish. We soon caught several more, plus a flounder, and more sand perch, which we started describing as "whatchamacallits" because we did not know what they were.

On the way back to the boat landing, as the sun was dying in a spectacular show, we saw something roiling the water. Whatever it was ignored my streamer, but when Ron cast his Dave Goforth bait, his rod bent. It was another small bluefish. Finally, I replaced my streamer with a Size Two chartreuse saltwater popper and dropped it into the roiling bluefish. If I let it sit for a minute at the end of the cast or fished it slow as I usually do for largemouth bass, nothing happened.

But if I kept the popper coming straight and popped it vigorously, splashing water a half-foot high, it drew violent strike after strike, each accompanied by loud noise. The fish apparently had difficulty getting their mouths around even the relatively small hook.

"This is fun even if I can't hook them," I told Ron.

But finally, I did catch one. My first bluefish on a fly rod! I went on to catch several more.

The next day, Ron and I again fished together and used the Dave Goforth Method to root out fish. This time, we caught small spotted sea trout after spotted sea trout.

The trout were all about twelve to thirteen inches long, so this time I picked up my light fly rod and, remembering something that Hubert Parrott said, tied a Charlie's bonefish fly to the end of my four-pound test leader. I soon caught my first fly rod sea trout.

186

Conrad and I fished together in the same spot the next day. This time, however, we caught dozens of white perch and only a few trout.

The six people in our party caught an incredible variety of fish: bluefish, chain pickerel, croaker, flounder, largemouth bass, puppy drum, sand perch, spot, trout, white perch, a catfish, several varieties of bream, and even a gar.

This, incidentally, was only a couple of weeks after Dave had died. I quietly wondered if Dave could see us. If he could, I knew he was smiling because he loved to help people catch fish.

A fishing trip I made to the same area less than two weeks later proved how fickle fishing in that area can be. Included in this party were Jerry Bledsoe, Wilt Browning, Gary McCann and Bill Wilkerson.

Bill, who had never fished this area before, was my partner. I had been telling him for years about how intriguing this kind of fishing could be. But, alas, a nor'easter blew in and we had much difficulty holding our boats still enough to fish. Bill and I, who both love to use fly rods, finally gave up on trying to cast our flies into the wind and switched to Dave's method. Using that, we managed to catch a few fish, both saltwater and freshwater species.

The next day, our group pulled our boats to Conaby Creek in an effort to find more peaceful waters. The creek, near Plymouth, is basically a freshwater stream and flows into the Roanoke River, which in turn empties into the Albemarle Sound.

Conaby is a beautiful creek that is sheltered on both sides with thick stands of towering cypresses and other trees. But on this day, most reaches of even this creek were too rough to fish without great effort. In desperation, I began fishing for bream in the few places I could cast my light fly rod. I

187

caught a few before something bigger took my small bream bug. It was a fair-size largemouth bass.

Bill—he and I were the only ones using fly rods—later pointed out to the others in our group that the biggest fish of the trip was caught on a fly.

Although Bill (see Chapter Nine) had fly fished over a wide area of North Carolina and in many other places, this was his first fly-fishing trip to Eastern North Carolina. I was afraid he was disappointed with the poor fishing we had experienced, especially because I had built up his expectations. But he wasn't.

He was so impressed with how fishy the water looked, he and one of his other fishing friends, Bob McCurley, returned to Eastern North Carolina a few weeks later. (Doris Dale and I were out of the country on vacation, so I couldn't go with them.)

But Bill and Bob, on this trip, chose to fish in salt water rather than in brackish water. They took only fly-fishing tackle and fished primarily for striped bass around the Highway 64–264 bridge that crosses Croatan Sound, and also in the more open water of the sound. They also fished, primarily for sea trout, in the shallow water in the southern part of Roanoke Sound and west of Oregon Inlet.

The two Guilford County anglers, who got to know each other while they were pilots at Piedmont Airlines and USAir, had fly fished in salt water in other places but never in North Carolina. Bob, who also once flew for Braniff, was the person who introduced Bill to fly fishing.

"I think I created a fly-fishing fanatic," jokes Bob, who is pretty much of a fanatic himself when it comes to fishing with long rods.

But because they were unfamiliar with North Carolina saltwater fly fishing, they retained the services of two guides: Bryan DeHart and Brian Horsley.

That was a wise decision, as it would be for anybody who has had no prior experience fly fishing in North Carolina salt water.

The two anglers used outfits similar to those many anglers use for fly fishing for largemouth bass: nine-foot rods matched for eight-weight lines.

"Most of the places we fished could have been fished in your boat," Bill told me later as he proudly showed me photographs of his and Bob's catches.

(At the time, I owned a fourteen-foot aluminum boat in which Bill and I often fished.)

"In fact," Bob, now retired, said, "we saw some small boats out there. Of course, you would have to watch the wind. That would be the main thing you have to watch out for."

Bill said, "We saw other fishermen who were using other types of tackle and we caught just as many or more on our fly rods as they were catching."

The water was relatively shallow, but the two anglers used sink tip lines most of the time when fishing for stripers. Only when fishing deeper water for stripers did they use fast sinking shooting heads.

They switched to floating lines when they encountered surface-schooling stripers. As you might expect, catching stripers on the top of the water was especially thrilling.

"Those striper came up and really boiled after our poppers," Bob recalled. "When you hooked one, two or three other stripers would try to take the popper away from the one that was hooked. It was crazy."

Bryan DeHart was their guide for the stripers; Brian Horsley guided them when they switched to sea trout fishing.

For their sea trout fishing, Bill and Bob used floating lines, neutral buoyancy lines or sink tip lines for the trout.

Most of the time, it was not necessary to make long casts. But accuracy was important, especially when the two anglers were fishing around pilings of the Roanoke Island Bridge where they caught many of their stripers. They had to get close to the pilings but not hit the pilings because of the barnacles on them. Also, once they hooked stripers they had to keep the fish away from the pilings, because the barnacles could slash their leaders.

The surface-schooling stripers that Bill and Bob caught were in open water.

Large Deceivers were the most effective streamers for stripers. Bill caught a few on a streamer called the Whistler. It was developed by California angler Dan Blanton for striper fishing in San Francisco Bay. It has lead eyes like the Clouser Minnow but is tied in a way that makes a whistling sound when cast. Hence, the name.

Most of Bob and Bill's sea trout were caught on medium-size Clousers.

In addition to striped bass and sea trout, Bob and Bill caught some small bluefish and a few other miscellaneous species. They released all their fish except for three trout that Bill brought home for his family to eat.

There are a number of small bays and other sheltered areas in the general area where Bob and Bill fished, if you want to try your hand at saltwater fly fishing but do not want to take a chance on fishing heavy water. Several boat ramps in the area are shown on maps published especially for anglers (see Appendix D).

Photo by Bob McCurley

Bill Wilkerson caught this striped bass on a fly in the Croatan Sound.

Stanley Winbourne, a Raleigh real estate broker, believes a nine-foot, nine-weight rod will handle just about any fish you are likely to catch in North Carolina sheltered brackish and salt water. If you do a lot of fly fishing in the big North Carolina freshwater lakes, chances are you already own such an outfit.

Stanley's opinion is not to be taken lightly. He has been fishing North Carolina brackish water and salt water with a fly rod for many years. He grew up in Wilmington and started out fishing for saltwater fish with spinning and bait-casting tackle. Sometimes, when he caught more fish than he needed, he sold the surplus.

As he matured, he worried about the decline of fish populations. "You start wondering if you are not a contributor to the decline," he says. For that reason, he quit selling fish. He also did something else.

"I started looking for ways to make my fishing more pleasurable without feeling that I had to catch so many fish," he recalls. "The idea of fishing not to keep score in numbers of fish you catch but keeping score in how much fun you had appealed to me more and more."

That's when Stanley decided to try using a fly rod to catch fish in brackish water and salt water around Wilmington.

Few people in those days used a fly rod in salt water. Consequently, Stanley could not find anyone to help him. He had to learn by trial and error.

He first tried fly fishing for bluefish.

"That was sort of an immediate way of finding out if fly fishing for saltwater fish worked," he says.

It worked, all right. It worked so well that Stanley began using his fly rod for other kinds of fish. Since then, he has caught many species.

As he had hoped, fly fishing offered him something that other types of fishing did not.

"It makes you think about more aspects of fishing than do most other kinds of fishing," he says. "You don't see very many fly fishermen talking to somebody or drinking a beer at the same time they are fishing, whereas if you are trolling, you can fish and drink a beer and listen to the radio and talk all at the same time.

"But if you are out in the marsh and wading and fly fishing, you pay attention to everything around you: how the tide is, how the wind is, and many other things. You know that all the details are more important than in other kinds of fishing. You have to pay attention to catch a fish, and when you catch one it just feels like you have accomplished more. Fly fishing [especially in salt water and brackish water] is, to some extent, a self-imposed handicap."

But not always, he adds.

"I have found that in 'skinny water' (shallow water) a fly rod is sometimes more effective. You can land your fly in the water without the big KER-PLUNK that a one-ounce lure makes. When you see a redfish (red drum) tailing up along the marsh, you can often put a fly out there about two feet in front of him without spooking him. Also, I believe that a fly, in certain instances, can be more realistic than other types of lures."

For example, Stanley has concluded that a fly rod can also be more deadly than other types of tackle when you need to fish very slowly—say when you are fishing for speckled trout when the water is cool.

"You can fish a fly real slow and make it look very realistic," he says. "When you fish spinning and casting lures real slow they just don't look so real."

193

Stanley thinks the biggest handicap that a fly fisherman faces in brackish water or salt water is the length of the cast he can make. No matter how good an angler is with a fly rod, Stanley points out, he just can't cast as far as an angler can with heavy spinning and baitcasting equipment.

"But that just makes a fly rod fisherman a better stalker of fish and brings another fascinating aspect to the sport," Stanley declares.

He thinks the Pamlico Sound area is especially good for "mixed-bag" fly fishing.

"That is a nice area," he says. "You might catch a large-mouth bass in the same place you catch a flounder in that water. That happens a lot when I fish that area with Fred Bonner."

(Fred Bonner is an outdoors writer and editor who grew up on the Pamlico Sound.)

Stanley agrees with Hubert Parrott that anglers interested in learning to fly fish in brackish and salt water should start out fishing for bluefish both because they are sometimes easy to catch and because they are exciting to catch.

"Bluefish will hit poppers that are about the size of a big bass bug, and they will strike the bug like a largemouth bass will strike it—only harder most of the time," he says. "And bluefish will almost always jump after they are hooked."

Stanley now makes most of his own bluefish poppers. Although bluefish will hit cork or balsa bugs, Stanley prefers to fashion bluefish popper bodies from soft material that will collapse when a bluefish smashes it. For hooks, he likes to use those that have long shanks and open bends. For popper tails, he usually uses synthetic feathers and adds some glitter. He attaches a short wire leader to the popper to prevent bluefish from severing his monofilament leader.

194

Also, like Hubert Parrot, Stanley prefers wading to fishing from a boat—in places where that is possible.

"Often, I will just anchor my boat and get out and wade," Stanley says.

He agrees with many other good fly rod anglers about what is the best all-around fly to use: the Clouser Minnow.

Some of Hubert's other favorites include Deceivers and, especially for speckled trout in weedy water, Chico's Bendbacks.

He likes light-colored flies in clear water and dark flies in dingy water.

He has caught many species of saltwater fish in sheltered salt water and many species of both freshwater fish and salt-water fish in brackish water. He has even caught a few striped bass in both brackish water and salt water. But, like Tom Kirkman of High Point, he has caught more stripers in swift water below dams than any other place.

One of Stanley's most memorable catches was a channel bass (red drum) that came close to breaking what was then a world's record on the type paraphernalia he was using.

He was fishing at Ocracoke and was using a leader with an eight-pound tippet.

"I very foolishly did not go in and weigh the fish as soon as I caught it," he says.

Instead, he left it in the boat, where it was exposed to the sun and air for hours.

When Stanley finally did weigh the fish, it weighed some twenty-two pounds, only a few ounces shy of breaking what was then the world's record for channel bass caught on a fly rod and eight-pound-test tippet.

He will always wonder if his fish would have made the record books if he had weighed it on certified scales before it dried out.

Stanley believes a person can take up brackish-water and light-saltwater fly fishing for a relatively modest outlay of money.

You can, of course, spend a thousand or more dollars on an outfit. But that is not necessary.

"Fred Bonner showed me a Berkley rod that he had bought—I'm scared to say how little he paid for it—and I couldn't believe how nice it was and how good it cast," Stanley says.

Stanley owns many top-flight reels—one of his favorites is the Orvis DXR—but often fishes with less expensive ones.

Although he started out using the trial-and-error method of saltwater fly fishing, he later made the acquaintances of Tom Earnhardt and Joel Arrington. Tom is a pioneer in North Carolina saltwater fly fishing, and Joel is an outstanding outdoor writer and photographer and a fine fly fisherman. Tom and Joel helped Stanley refine his saltwater fly fishing.

Fly fishing resulted in Stanley buying himself one of the best Christmas presents a fly fisherman could receive: a major interest in a fishing operation in the tropics.

Stanley's wife, Alice, was indirectly responsible for Stanley's purchase. In the 1960s, she was an artist with Brown University archaeological expeditions based in Guatemala. When she and others on the archaeological teams got time off, they often visited Belize, a country between Guatemala and Mexico.

She introduced Stanley to Belize.

"At first, I started going down to dive on the reefs," Stanley recalls.

He fell in love with the beautiful country. Its people, although of many races and many diverse mixed races, live in peace and harmony.

Stanley, on his diving excursions, saw many varieties of tropical and sub-tropical fish—species that he knew were prized by anglers. This led him to the conclusion that Belize had other appealing characteristics in addition to its people, its climate, its beauty and its fine diving; it was the perfect place for fishing, especially fly fishing.

As a result, he started taking his fishing equipment on trips to Belize and using techniques he had learned while fishing in North Carolina brackish water and salt water. He caught many fish—permit, tarpon, snook, bonefish, barracuda, mutton snapper, and other saltwater fish—mostly on fly fishing rods. He caught freshwater species in the rivers that flow down from the mountains and caught these, too, mostly on fly tackle.

Later, to help pay his expenses, he escorted groups of anglers on trips to the tropical paradise.

Then, on Christmas Eve of 1993, Stanley and some other investors bought a fishing operation, including lodging and boarding facilities, in Belize.

"It was a Christmas present to myself," he says.

He now goes to Belize every chance he gets.

But he also continues to fish North Carolina fresh, brackish and salt water—much of the time with a fly rod—at every opportunity.

Shad, another fish that can sometimes be caught on a fly rod in Eastern North Carolina needs mentioning even though few fly rod anglers fish for it in this state.

Why we North Carolina fly rod anglers don't fish for them is puzzling, because shad fishing is a popular early springtime sport of fly rod anglers in many other states on both coasts.

The only fishermen I know who have caught shad on a fly rod are John Baskervill of Greensboro and Vince Davis of Lewisville in Forsyth County.

And John confesses that his fish were caught on a fly rod almost as an afterthought.

John and a friend were fishing for shad with spinning rods in the Cape Fear river when it happened. After they had caught enough fish on spinning tackle to let them know the shad were in a biting mood, John picked up his fly rod to see what would happen.

His reel was loaded with deep sinking line that he had made himself from lead-core trolling line. He had tied a few shad flies from patterns that he had seen in books and used one of those.

He caught several shad.

That has been a long time ago. He has not fished for shad since. In fact, he rarely even uses a sinking line now.

Vince Davis has used a fly rod to catch shad in more recent years. His in-laws live in the Rocky Mount area and, when he visits them, he sometimes fishes the Tar River. In the early spring, he catches shad on a white Clouser Swimming Minnow. He uses a floating line, but the Clouser sinks deep enough to reach the fish.

Shad are an anadromous species, which means that they spend part of their time in salt water and part in fresh water. Typically, they can be caught in freshwater streams such as the Tar River only in early spring and mid-spring when they make their spawning run.

The shad run is a cause for great celebration in much of Eastern North Carolina. Both varieties of shad (hickory and American, or white shad) and their roe are considered delicacies. Besides, both are sporting to catch, and anglers using spinning and casting gear line the banks or fish from boats.

North Carolina streams in which shad can be caught when they make their spring spawning runs are: the Black River, Cape Fear River, Contentnea Creek, Neuse River, Pee Dee River, Pitchkettle Creek, Tar River, Trent River, White Oak River, and similar streams that flow into the ocean or saltwater sounds.

In other states where fly fishing for shad is more widely practiced than in North Carolina, flies that have a little flash and some color are popular. So are spinner flies. Because shad are often caught in deep, swift water, including water that is swollen from spring rains, sinking fly lines, or at least deep sinking flies, are often used.

There is one other thing you should know about fishing in brackish water or salt water in Eastern North Carolina or anywhere in the world, for that matter. If you aren't careful, the salinity can play havoc with your equipment. This is especially true if you use equipment designed primarily for freshwater fishing. But it is also true of even equipment made for saltwater fishing.

This doesn't mean you have to buy special tackle to fish in brackish water and salt water. It does mean, however, that you should wash your rods and reels in fresh water at the end of a day's fishing. It is a good idea also to rinse your poppers and streamers in fresh water. Salt can rust even those hooks that are designed especially for use in salt water. At the end of each trip to Eastern North Carolina, you should not only bathe your equipment in fresh water but also lubricate the metal parts.

I forgot to do this after one trip to the Pungo River. The next time I went fishing, my expensive Orvis reel was frozen and I couldn't turn it. It was locked so tight, I had difficulty even removing the spool.

After an hour or so of work and generous use of a spray lubricant and reel grease, I managed to restore the reel (which, being a gift, has a lot of sentimental value to me) to working order. I have since caught many fish on it in both fresh water and brackish water, and hope to catch many more before John or Conrad inherit it, after I have used it for the last time.

Chapter Fifteen

Bugging Fish at Night

If you are like many other anglers, you love to fish so much that you will go fishing even when the weather is so hot that your clothes stick to your body and sweat stings your eyes and you are almost too debilitated to cast. But most anglers prefer to fish when temperatures are more pleasant.

Besides, during the hot summer, North Carolina public lakes are usually crowded with hordes of water skiers, jet skiers, bass boaters, speed boaters, and other pleasure seekers—especially on weekends. If you are a fly fisherman, there is yet another reason for avoiding public waters during the middle of the summer: fish are often in deep water, and it is more difficult to get a fly down to them.

So what is a fly fisherman to do when temperatures soar? Sleep during the day and fish at night, that's what. Many species—especially bream and other panfish and striped bass, largemouth bass, and smallmouth bass—often move into shallow water on summer nights. Then you can catch them on or near the top. Night, in fact, is about the only time in the hot summer when you can usually count on catching largemouth bass on a topwater lure.

Many anglers who use baitcasting and spinning gear learned this a long time ago. Surprisingly, however, you still don't see many fly rod anglers on the water at night. In avoiding the dark, those anglers miss some fascinating and often fantastic fly fishing.

I, too, started out night fishing with spinning and bait-casting equipment exclusively—mainly because I didn't know how to use a fly rod then. When I was a young boy, I often fished Lake Wylie for largemouth bass at night—frequently catching fish. Later I fished baitcasting tackle at night on other lakes: Hickory, James, Jordan, Kerr, Norman, and the Yadkin River impoundments. Even after I took up fly fishing, I did not think about using the long rod at night. I usually fished a Jitterbug lure on either baitcasting or spin-casting equipment.

The reason I usually fished a Jitterbug was simple. Although bass will sometimes hit just about any lure at night, a noisy topwater lure is the most exciting—and often the most effective—to use. Oddly, bass seem to prefer a black lure over a light-colored one at night. Some anglers speculate that a black lure makes a better silhouette against the sky than does a light-colored lure.

Even saltwater fish seem to prefer black flies at night as Bill Wilkerson and Bob McCurley, learned. It was their first try at saltwater fishing (see Chapter Fourteen) in North Carolina, and they had success daytime and nighttime. At night, they fished primarily for striped bass. Although they caught stripers on several different kinds of streamers, the fish seemed to prefer black Deceivers after dark.

You don't have to travel to the coast to catch fish at night. No matter where you live in North Carolina, you can usually find some good night fly fishing close to home.

I remember an especially interesting night fishing trip with Jack Bilyeu. He and I fished a Greensboro lake when the moon was full. An occasional cloud drifted across the face of the moon, bringing what seemed like total darkness to our corner of the world.

Photo by Bill Wilkerson

Bob McCurley, left, and Bryan DeHart display striper caught at night on a black streamer.

As the night wore on, we noticed something strange. The fish hit our black Jitterbugs much better when the moon was obscured than they did when it was out.

Even after I learned to use a fly rod, it still took me several years to reason that if bass hit topwater spinning and baitcasting lures at night, they would hit fly rod popping bugs at night. None of my friends who used fly rods ever mentioned that they had caught fish at night on fly rods, even though I later learned that some of them had. So when I first began fly fishing, I left my fly rod at home when I went fishing at night.

This changed one summer after I fished a Greensboro-area lake with a neighbor, Bill Jerome. We left home late in the afternoon, but it was still daylight when we launched my boat. I, of course, fished my fly rod during the afternoon but planned to switch to my baitcasting outfit for the night fishing.

Just before the sun disappeared, bass began to smash my home-made black popping bug. I became so busy landing fish that I forgot to switch to my baitcasting outfit and a black Jitterbug after night closed in. The bass continued to hit the popper throughout the night. Since then, when fishing at night, I always start out with my fly rod, switching to other types of gear only as a last resort.

There are nights, of course, when other types of gear will outfish the fly rod. But if you are even half-way proficient and the fish are cooperating at all, you will usually catch some fish on the long rod after nightfall.

A mid-August jaunt Greg Campbell and I made to a Guilford County lake was typical of my night fly fishing experiences. Greg is a good friend to have because he can take you fishing in lakes that you could not get to fish if he did not invite you. By day during the week, he is a metal fabricator. By night and on weekends, he is a "limnologist." That means he practices "limnology," which my ancient *Webster's Collegiate Dictionary* defines as "the scientific study of fresh waters, esp. ponds and lakes...."

What Greg does as a limnologist is advise residents of private community lakes about the health of the fish populations in the lakes and what can be done to correct problems. In return for Greg's advice, the lake residents give him fishing privileges.

That's how he and I came to fish this particular lake on a beautiful starlit summer night. Greg had already launched his boat and was fishing near the boat dock when I arrived just as the sun was expiring. Although temperatures had come close to setting a record high earlier that day, the breeze blowing off the lake held the promise of sweet relief.

I loaded my nine-foot fly rod and fly box in Greg's boat. Greg would be fishing with spinning and baitcasting rods—his tackle of choice.

After I climbed into the boat, Greg eased down a shoreline. He made only a few casts with an artificial worm before saying, "There he is!"

He set the hook and reeled in a medium-size bass. He gently placed the bass in the boat's live well. He would later measure and tag that bass and release it along with the others that we caught.

I used a topwater bass bug. Greg caught several bass on his artificial worm before I finally heard a commotion in the direction of where I thought my bug was floating in the blackness. I landed a small bass. By now, the night was pleasantly cool.

As you might expect, Greg knows the lakes he studies so well that he can tell you where things are even when he can't see them.

"There's a wall over there," he said as he used his electric motor to move his boat silently down the lake. "Cast over there. There's usually a fish around the wall."

After squinting, I finally made out the faint outline of a concrete wall and dropped my bug as close to it as I could.

Immediately, a fish made a thrashing sound as it hit the bug. I was too late setting the hook and missed the fish.

We fished until after midnight and caught more than a dozen bass. Greg caught most of his bass on an artificial worm. I caught my bass and a couple of big bluegill bream on a large popper. All the fish, including the bream, made loud splashes when they hit.

Speaking of bream, some books on fishing say that blue-gills and their relatives do not feed at night. That's not true—especially if you're talking about our North Carolina bream. They will often hit a popper so violently at night that you think they are bass.

Some of my friends and I used to fish luminous poppers for bream at night. We beamed a flashlight on the bugs until the paint glowed and then fished until the paint dimmed. Then we used a flashlight to reactivate the paint. In recent years, it has been hard to find luminous bugs where I live and apparently some other places, too. Jim Bass of Lumber-ton has found a way to solve that problem. He cuts up glow-in-the-dark condoms—no off-color remarks, please—and glues the fragments to his regular poppers.

At night, you should fish your bream bug slow to give the fish a chance to find it. But when you do pop the bug, make enough noise to draw attention.

Some fly rod anglers also fish for landlocked striped bass at night. Here, too, fly rod anglers can learn something from their baitcasting buddies. A favorite tactic of baitcasters who fish for stripers at night is to use a large Rebel, Redfin or similar artificial bait and retrieve it steadily across the top of the water so that it leaves a wake like that which a snake or frog leaves as it swims. Fly rod anglers who fish for stripers at night can get a similar effect by using a large salt-water slider popper, retrieving it in long steady strips.

Many good largemouth and smallmouth bass fishermen fish a topwater lure or fly rod bug slow no matter what time of the day it is. It's a good idea to fish even slower at night, yet still work the lure or bass bug so that it makes enough racket to inform the fish where it is. So let your bug sit still for a few seconds at the end of a cast. Then retrieve it about six feet, popping it energetically enough to make it sound off. Then let it sit still again for a few seconds, repeating these steps until you get it back to the boat. Sometimes a bass will thrash at a popping bug in the dark several times before hitting it. Talk about heart-stopping!

Once, as mentioned earlier, just about everybody who fished at night used Jitterbugs or other topwater lures. That has now changed and more anglers fish underwater lures, even at night. Greg Campbell is among those anglers. He catches a lot of bass on artificial worms at night. Once more, the fly rodder can learn something from the baitcaster. A fly rod angler can use flies that look a lot like artificial worms and have similar actions. These include Clouser Minnows, Whitlock's Water Pups, Woolly Buggers, weighted Marabou Leeches, and weighted Marabou Muddlers and similar things.

When using underwater streamers, fly rod anglers can take still another page from artificial worm fishermen. Artificial worm anglers have learned that even the worm is more effective if it is fished so that it makes a little noise. So when their artificial worms crawl over a rock or twig, creating a little racket, they get ready for a strike. Some artificial worm fishermen use weights that contain rattles or insert little rattles inside the worms so that the worm makes a noise even when it is crawling across smooth territory.

What does this tell fly rod anglers? That bass will often grab a streamer or other underwater fly as it falls off a twig or otherwise creates a noise. It also tells them that a spinner fly, an underwater fly rod lure that makes a fuss, is another good thing to use at night.

Some fly rod anglers who tie their own flies for night fishing make them semi-weedless (see Chapter Three). You can also buy weedless bugs and flies. The reason for using these, of course, is that you hang up more often at night because it is more difficult to see even when the moon is full.

And it is better if only one of you uses a fly rod while the other uses spinning or baitcasting tackle. Otherwise, you could spend a lot of your time snagging your partner's line on your back cast.

And because you can't see as well at night as you can in the daytime, the night can be fraught with danger for an angler who is not cautious.

For safety's sake, it is better to fish with a partner at night.

There are other things you can do to make night fishing safer:

• Wear your life jacket instead of just having it handy as many anglers do during the daytime.

• Be careful when you move around in the boat. It is easier to fall out of the boat when you can't see.

• Keep lures in your tackle box with the lid latched so you won't spill the contents if you knock it over, or worse, hook yourself.

• Keep other equipment stored neatly in your boat so you won't stumble over it in the darkness and topple out.

• Take along several good flashlights. Try to avoid shining them in your eyes, though, because it takes time to get accustomed to the dark again. Also, if you accidentally shine your light on the water, it could spook the fish.

• Arrange your tackle so that you can change flies with a minimum of effort and noise. It is easier to hook yourself when visibility is poor. Moreover, while some kinds of noise in the water attract fish, banging on your boat can frighten them.

• Be careful when you cast, because you are more likely to hook yourself or your partner when you can't see well. I don't like to fly fish, even in the day time, with a partner who doesn't wear glasses. If you hook your partner anywhere else except in the eyes—well, almost anywhere else—it will usually not do much permanent harm.

• If you are fishing on a lake where there is even occasional night traffic, switch on your boat lights.

• Use caution when you are moving your boat from one place to the other, especially under the power of your gasoline motor. You've read or heard of the tragic consequences of people running into boat docks and piers at night.

• You should not drink while operating your boat in the daytime. It is even more foolish to consume alcohol in a boat at night.

• Keep an eye on where you are. It is easy to get lost in the dark—even on a lake that you know well. Fogs can form quickly at night, making it difficult to find your way back to the boat landing.

There is a special charm and mystery to fishing in the dark, especially on a clear night. Stars seem so close you feel you could cast your lure to them. Insects buzz dreamily. Whip-poor-wills cry in the distance. Lightning bugs blink and trail yellow luminous streaks in the air. Owls hoot mournfully. Ducks quack sleepily. Frogs bellow. When the moon is full, a mist-covered lake looks like an impressionist painting. At night on the water, the world is at peace. Worries seem far away.

You never know what you will see at night. Sometimes when you hang up and go to retrieve your fly or popper and turn on your flashlight to determine where you are snagged, you will see two eyes glowing and find yourself face to face with a raccoon. I've had this to happen several times.

Greg made the night I fished with him even more interesting by hanging a "black light" lamp on the side of the boat so that it illuminated his fluorescent line as he retrieved. The line glowed and did a ghostly dance in the black light. I replaced the first few feet of my fly leader with fluorescent line, and it looked especially magical as I retrieved. It became an eerie but colorful snake twitching through midair.

North Carolina lakes are among some of the best in the world to fish at night. Maybe we'll meet on one of them after sundown one night soon, and you'll be using your fly rod. Until then, sweet dreams of fly fishing in the dark.

Chapter Sixteen

Fishing Behind the Post Office and in Belly Boats

Want to know a place close to your home where you can catch big bass and panfish on your fly rod while fishing all day in serenity?

Pssst. Come a little closer so nobody else can hear: Get permission to fish the "Little Pond Behind the Post Office."

Just about every year, I catch my first bass of the year in one of these ponds. And I usually catch my first fly rod bass of the year in one of them, as well as my largest bream of the year.

One year, I fished well into spring and in many kinds of water—Eastern North Carolina, several Piedmont lakes, and even some mountain waters—without catching even one bass on a fly rod. I caught some on other kinds of tackle but not even a small one on a fly rod. I was beginning to wonder if I had become an impotent fly fisherman.

Then John Peterson, a friend who owns a getaway cottage on a Little Pond Behind the Post Office, invited me to fish the pond. The pond has some big bream and crappie, in addition to bass. So I carried only my seven-foot fly rod, hoping to catch one of the panfish. Given my luck so far that year, I didn't think there was much use to fish for bass with a fly rod.

Doris Dale and John's wife, Mary Jane, sat on the porch overlooking the lake and talked while John and I fished. I tied a tiny bream bug to the end of the four-pound tippet of my leader while John eased the boat within casting distance of some overhanging willows.

"Why don't you cast under those willows," John suggested, pointing to some low hanging limbs. "It's a good place for bream."

That's what I did, throwing sidearm to keep the bream bug from hanging up on the bushes.

The splat the bug made as it landed on the water was followed immediately by a loud splash, and a fish cleared the water. It was not a bream. It was a medium-size largemouth bass that felt, on the light rod, much larger.

I was so thrilled that the ham in me, which always lurks just below the surface anyway, came out. I yelled for Mary Jane and Doris Dale to watch. The bass played a supporting role—or maybe it was a starring role—by jumping several times. The four-pound tippet withstood the stress and I at last landed the bass—with John's help. To reward the bass for helping me perform, I released it.

On another day, John and I fished the same pond and caught bass after bass on our fly rods on a sweltering July day. We also caught some nice bream.

The bass smashed poppers until noon when the sun beat down from a cloudless sky and temperatures soared to above ninety degrees Fahrenheit, forcing us to come to our senses and abandon the Pond Behind the Post Office to search for a restaurant that served iced tea.

I took with me the memory of a sensational morning of fishing. I also took away the memory of something unusual that had happened.

Photo by John Ellison

Author caught this largemouth bass on a "Pond Behind the Post Office." It was released after photo was made.

A bass that John and I estimated to be ten inches long hit my bass bug. As I was stripping the bass in, another bass, about a two-pounder, tried to eat my bass. I quickly landed my fish and, after waiting a minute or so, released it.

"I wonder if I saved that bass by catching it?" I asked John.

John didn't dignify that with an answer. Later, as we ate barbecue sandwiches and sipped refreshing tea from frosted glasses, we agreed that we had never seen one bass try to catch a fellow bass that had been hooked. We had seen bass go after hooked bream, but never a hooked bass. All the bass and bream we caught that morning had been healthy, so that bass with cannibalistic tendencies could not have been desperate for food.

A Pond Behind the Post Office is, by the way, not only a good place to catch fish. It is a good place to learn to fly fish.

So where do you find Little Ponds Behind the Post Office? At the risk of boring those who read my two earlier fishing books, *Tar Heel Angler* and *Bass Fishing in North Carolina*, here's the answer.

The phrase "Pond Behind the Post Office" was created one day when the Reverend Sam Sox—"Preacher Sam," as he was affectionately known to his fishing buddies—caught a largemouth bass that weighed more than nine pounds. He was naturally proud of the big fish and went by the basement of Phipps Hardware in downtown Greensboro, then a favorite hangout of anglers, to show off the fish.

Bobby Andrew, who worked in the fishing tackle department in the hardware store basement, asked Preacher Sam where he caught the fish.

Preacher Sam, pastor of Greensboro's First Lutheran Church at the time, could not tell a falsehood. Yet he did not want to reveal where he really caught the fish. So he just mumbled, and Bobby guessed the truth.

"Oh," Bobby said, "so you caught it in the little Pond Behind the Post Office, did you?"

Preacher Sam had caught the fish in a privately-owned farm pond. Bodie McDowell, then outdoors writer for the *Greensboro Daily News*, heard the story and wrote about it.

From then on, when Preacher Sam caught a big fish in a farm pond, Bodie duly reported that the minister caught it in the "Pond Behind the Post Office."

Some of Bodie's readers tried to find the Pond Behind the Post Office. Bodie received a number of calls about the pond.

"There's a pond not too far from the McLeansville Post Office," one caller declared, referring to a Guilford County community east of Greensboro. "That's where that preacher fishes, isn't it?"

Another caller complained to Bodie, "I've lived in Greensboro all my life and if there's a pond behind the post office, I don't know anything about it!"

There may be no pond behind the post office in downtown Greensboro, but if there were, chances are that you could catch fish in it.

Because only owners and guests usually fish farm ponds, there is little pressure on the ponds, and the fish are often plentiful, and many grow to be huge.

How do you get permission to fish the ponds?

Answer: Make friends with a farmer who owns a farm pond, or at least make friends with someone who knows someone who owns one or more farm ponds. That way, maybe you will get permission to fish one of the ponds.

At one time, you could often get permission to fish a farm pond just by walking up to a farmer's door, knocking, and asking. If you make the right kind of impression, this still may work occasionally. But not often. Crime has made even the most neighborly of farmers cautious.

Still, there are thousands of farm ponds in North Carolina. So chances are that you know someone who owns one or at least you probably know somebody who knows somebody else who owns one.

Farm ponds, of course, weren't built primarily for fishing. They were built for irrigation. Yet most farmers stock their lakes with bream and largemouth bass. Some farmers also stock crappie and catfish.

A few farmers won't allow anybody to fish their ponds. Most, however, will oblige anglers they know or anglers who have the right introduction and are decent and who follow some rules of common courtesy.

Among the rules are:

• Never fish a pond without the owner's authorization.

• If the owner likes to eat fish, offer to share your catch. It helps to clean the fish before handing them over.

• Treat a pond as if you owned it. Don't litter or do anything else that you wouldn't do to your own pond.

• Don't be a hog. If you have a good catch, resist the temptation to go back the next day. It is easy to overfish a small pond.

• Don't take anybody else to a farm pond that you have permission to fish unless the pond owner says it is okay.

• Even if you have an open invitation, don't fish a pond unless the owner knows you are going to fish it.

So how do you fish a farm pond once you have access to one?

Preacher Sam, one of the state's foremost authorities on farm pond fishing, had this advice: fish a farm pond just about like you fish any other lake.

So when you are fishing with a fly rod, you fish it about like you would fish a fly rod anywhere else for bass: floating and shallow running flies in the spring and fall, and early in the morning and late in the afternoon and at night, and deep sinking flies such as Clouser Minnows in cooler weather and during the day in the hot summer. The same general rules hold true for bream and crappie. Only, of course, you fish smaller bugs and flies for bream and only sinking flies for crappie.

"If you take any large lake and cut off a cove of it, you'd have a farm pond—in the sense that what you find in a farm pond, you'll also find in that particular cove," Preacher Sam said. "There are areas where you'll find bream. There are areas where you'll find small bass. There are areas where you'll find big bass."

So if you learn to fish a fly rod well on a farm pond, chances are you will be able to catch fish about anywhere else you fish a fly rod.

On occasion, Preacher Sam used a boat to fish a farm pond. But he preferred to fish from the bank.

"It requires you to be a little stealthy," Preacher Sam said. "You've got to creep around. Even the crack of a little twig may alarm the fish."

Learning to wade quietly or move silently along the bank of a farm pond will stand you in good stead when you fish for mountain trout.

Many farmers clear the banks of their ponds of bushes and trees so that a beginning fly rod angler can fish without fear of hanging up. Others, however, are overgrown in the very spot where you are likely to catch big fish. So this gives you an opportunity to learn roll casts, side-arm casts and other techniques that will also come in handy when you fish mountain streams for trout.

Paul Salazar has found the perfect watercraft for an angler who would prefer to fish Little Ponds Behind the Post Office from a boat rather than from the bank.

But before learning what kind of boat this is, you should know a little of Paul's interesting background.

He is a fine fly rod fisherman—something he may not ever have become if he had not attended West Point Military Academy, where he sometimes got into trouble.

Paul uses a "belly boat" to fish for bass and bream and anything else that he might catch on a fly in farm ponds. A belly boat is built around a truck tire inner tube. The tube is encased in sturdy fabric. A seat attached to the cover holds the angler in the middle of the belly boat so that the angler's legs and feet hang down in the water. The cover also has places for an angler to store tackle.

Swim fins enable the angler to propel the belly boat around the water.

So what does this have to do with Paul's experiences at West Point? A lot, that's what.

Paul entered the army in 1963. Two years later, he received one of the few appointments that West Point gives to enlisted soldiers each year.

At West Point, Paul received "demerits," or marks for some infraction of rules.

"They say Eisenhower set the record for having the most demerits of anybody up until his days at the Academy," Paul says.

Then he jokingly adds, "But I think I broke his record."

Photo by Buck Paysour

Paul Salazar fishes from a belly boat in a farm pond.

Don't misunderstand. Although Paul was (and still is) a free spirit, he wasn't such a bad cadet. Even a minor infraction can earn a cadet a demerit at West Point. A cadet can receive one if his buttons are not polished exactly right. He can receive one if his shoes aren't shined well enough to reflect the sun. He can receive one if he doesn't shave closely enough.

Anyway, Paul was supposed to be confined to his quarters while serving his demerits. But he sometimes slipped out to visit fellow cadets. One cadet he visited was a fly fisherman and a fly tyer. Paul was fascinated as he watched the cadet create counterfeit insects from feather, thread, hook and other materials. Paul decided that would be fun to do, and he asked the other cadet to give him fly-tying lessons. The other cadet not only did that but also took Paul up on the roof of their quarters and taught him how to fly cast.

So when Paul graduated from West Point in 1969, he had not only learned how to be an officer and a gentleman, but he also had learned the gentlemanly art of fly fishing.

War temporarily interrupted his fly fishing, however. He was sent to Vietnam where he commanded an airborne company.

When he returned from Vietnam, he resumed fly fishing. Fly fishing changed his life in many ways. It led to his becoming a Tar Heel. A California native, he fell in love with North Carolina and North Carolina's fly fishing while serving at Fort Bragg. So he remained in the state after leaving the army in 1975.

North Carolina's good fly fishing was not the only thing that attracted Paul to the state. He fell in love with a North Carolina woman, Amy Wood of Yadkin County.

He and Amy moved to Guilford County after they were married in 1981, and Paul went to work at AT&T as an engineer.

He brought his belly boats—he had taken up belly boating about the time he left the army in 1975—with him when he moved.

In Guilford County, he joined the Nat Greene fly fishing club and subsequently was elected its president and has taught fly-tying lessons for the club.

On this particular warm spring day, Paul has chosen a pond near his Pleasant Garden home to fish from his belly boat.

"I sometimes wear waders, especially when it's cold," Paul says as he straps on his swim fins, climbs into his belly boat, picks up his fly rod, and slips into the water.

But today he is going to fish "wet," in walking shorts.

"My waders have sprung a leak and I haven't had time to patch them," he says.

After maneuvering his boat out a few feet from the bank, Paul begins making flawless casts. Soon, he catches and releases a nice bluegill bream.

Using his feet and the fins on his feet to propel the boat, he eases to a new position and continues to cast. A belly boat has several advantages over more conventional watercraft, he tells me as I observe him from shore.

"It makes less noise," he explains. "And it's lower in the water so that fish can not see you as easily as they can if you are in a regular boat."

Also, it is easier to launch a belly boat than it is to launch a bass boat or other larger craft. Accordingly, you can fish ponds and lakes that have no boat launching ramps.

And a belly boat costs less than a more conventional boat. You can buy a basic one for less than $100. The more deluxe models cost around $200—still a far cry from what you have to pay for most regular fishing boats. Most mail order companies that deal in fly fishing tackle sell belly boats (see Appendix B). So do many local outdoor stores.

"The water is really nice today," Paul says several time as he fishes on this balmy day.

The fishing is good, too.

In just a short while, he hooks and lands several other bream and a couple of largemouth bass, releasing each fish.

He catches most of his fish on a Clouser Minnow. He agrees with other good fly rod anglers who think the Clouser is the best all-around streamer.

Paul sports a handsome dark full beard, which he grew shortly after leaving the army. The beard ended his military career once and for all.

The Army once approached him about joining the reserves.

He declined.

"They wouldn't let me keep my beard," he says with a chuckle.

Paul is fortunate to have permission to fish many farm ponds in his belly boats. He almost always catches fish.

As my friend, John Ellison, says, "I think the day is coming when you'll have to go to a private lake to find good fishing."

I hope John is wrong.

Yet even now, many of the largest bass and bream caught in North Carolina each year are caught in farm ponds and other private ponds and lakes. A state record largemouth bass was caught in a farm pond near Charlotte. But it was not caught on a fly rod.

John Ellison, by the way, owns one of the best farm lakes I have ever fished.

Where is it?

That's another rule that you should follow if you are lucky enough to get an invitation to fish a farm pond or other private lake: Don't ever tell anybody where the pond is. If pressed by your fishing buddies to tell them where you made your big catches, try the answer that Bodie McDowell and Bobby Andrew created for the Reverend Sam Sox.

Say that you caught the fish in "The Pond Behind the Post Office."

But I can give you a hint about where John Ellison's lake is. It's not behind the Post Office. It's a few miles from it.

Photo by Howard Gold

Johnny Owens, one of the last of the old-time fishing guides on Currituck Sound, died accidentally on the sound he loved.

Afterword

Death of a Guide and a Sound

Johnny Owens' ashes were scattered over Currituck Sound.

That was as it should have been. Now, the Currituck County hunting and fishing guide will forever be a part of the vast body of water that was so much a part of his life—a body of water that, in the end, claimed his life.

For many years to come, Johnny will also be a part of the memories of the many duck hunters and bass fishermen that he guided over the years.

During most of the years that Johnny guided, Currituck Sound's waters were among the world's finest for large-mouth bass fishing—especially bass fishing with a fly rod. Johnny loved guiding for all kinds of anglers but had a special affection for fly fishermen.

In recent years, however, fewer and fewer anglers have fished the sound. The reason: development, runoff from agricultural chemicals and other pollution and the intrusion of too much salt water have just about ruined the large-mouth bass fishing.

Johnny was a hard worker. He had to be. He had fourteen children. Even when he guided regularly, he did many different kinds of labor between duck hunting and sports fishing bookings to make ends meet. As fewer and fewer anglers and hunters made the trip to the sound, he turned more of his attention to enterprises other than guiding. Commercial fishing was one thing that he did. That is how he died.

In the gathering dusk one day in the fall of 1993, he went out to check the nets he had set in the sound. He did not return as scheduled. Upon learning that he was overdue, some of his fellow fishermen, several of whom had also been sports fishing guides at one time, went out to search. They discovered his capsized skiff, the same skiff that he had used the last time I fished with him, tied to a duck blind. The next morning, Johnny's friends found his body. The Coast Guard declared his death an accidental drowning.

Doris Dale and I were out of town and did not hear of Johnny's death until after his funeral. So we did not get to Currituck to say a final good-bye. In a way, I'm glad of that. I prefer to remember Johnny as he was the last time I fished with him.

I also prefer to remember the sound as it was when I first met Johnny a quarter-century ago. Then the sound was pristine and the bass fishing wonderful. Even today, the sound is one of the world's most beautiful and unusual bodies of water. Sunrises over the sound are awe-inspiring.

Yet, to me and other fly fishermen, the sound is only a ghost of what it once was. On the Currituck Sound of my memories, bass smash my popping bug often enough each day for me to catch my limit. Also on the sound of my memories, innumerable flights of Canada geese etch their Vs across the heavens. Ospreys dip and wheel on unseen thermal columns. Rafts of wild ducks bob on the sound's water and fly back and forth across its marshes. An occasional bald eagle soars overhead. Raccoons do not even stop their hunting when your skiff passes close by. Deer populate the sound's woods and marshes. Swans float regally in the ponds off the sound's main body. You still see some of these things on the sound, of course, but they are not as common as they were just a few years ago.

On its east side, only a splinter of land known as Currituck Banks separates the sound from the "Graveyard of the Atlantic," which gets its name from the many shipwrecks that have occurred there. During the years I regularly fished the sound, it was one of the few places in the world where you could catch largemouth bass while listening to the ocean's roar. I remember fly fishing for largemouth bass with Cecil Martin—Johnny Owens was our guide as I recall—on a fog-shrouded day when we could hear mournful blasts of fog horns on vessels plying the shipping lanes of the Atlantic.

The sound is fed primarily by the North Landing River, a freshwater stream that flows out of Virginia. But the river is lethargic and does not have the strength to flush out all the sea water that seeps into the sound through Oregon Inlet on Albemarle Sound to the south. This makes Currituck brackish, which means it is part fresh water and part ocean water. When I first started fishing the sound, it had just enough salinity to attract saltwater fish such as flounder. Yet its waters were also fresh enough to sustain abundant numbers of freshwater fish such as bream, crappie, and largemouth bass.

I remember a morning when Bill Black and Skipper Bowles, who regularly made trips to the sound with our group, caught their limits of largemouth bass on fly rod poppers and other artificial lures. Then their guide bought them minnows, and they returned to the sound after lunch and caught a tubful of flounder. That night we kidded Bill, then a young banker, and Skipper, one of North Carolina's best known sportsmen and political figures, about going fishing for largemouth bass and catching flounder.

"Don't knock it until you've tried it," Skipper said, flashing his engaging smile.

Off and on during Currituck's history, storms that frequently rake the North Carolina Outer Banks have blasted inlets through Currituck Banks, allowing the Atlantic Ocean to pour into the sound. Each time, another storm eventually struck Currituck Banks at just the right angle, sealing the inlet again. This last happened in 1828 when a hurricane closed New Currituck Inlet. Before it was shut, New Currituck Inlet remained open nearly a hundred years, long enough for many saltwater species such as oysters, to flourish in the sound.

Years later, when I fished the sound, you would sometimes catch largemouth bass over ancient oyster shells. You knew this was true because the guide's shoving pole would make crunching sounds as it rammed the bottom.

Now, Currituck is too salty for freshwater fish. You have to fish hard to catch even a few largemouth bass—the fish that once drew anglers from all over the world to the sound.

As a result, the party of eight to ten anglers with whom I fished the sound twice a year, just about every year, hardly ever makes the trip anymore. Two years ago, I did persuade some of my friends to make the trip one more time for nostalgia's sake. It was to be the last time I ever fished with Johnny Owens.

The camaraderie is warm as we fishermen sit on the porch of Barrett's Hunting and Fishing Lodge and look out over the sound, sip drinks, and rig our tackle for tomorrow's fishing. It is our first trip back to Currituck in several years and, for a while, at least, it is as if nothing has changed. But we know in our hearts that many things are different. My friends and I have come to fish Currituck for what may be our final time. We have come, not because we expect to catch fish. We have come, rather, to relive memories of a time that will most likely never be repeated, a time when you could just about always catch your limit of bass. Something else is different. When we first began fishing Currituck Sound some quarter century earlier, most of us were young and death seemed so remote we hardly gave it a second thought. Now we are older and several of our friends who once made this trip with us are gone: Skipper Bowles, Bob Ingram, Duncan Stephenson, Claibourne Darden, Bynum Hines....

Other things are different, too. Hugh and Irene Carpenter, who bought Barrett's Hunting and Fishing Lodge from Evelyn Barrett after Ed Barrett died, say bass fishing in the sound is poor and has been for several years. That was something we already knew before we left Greensboro.

In the late afternoon, as dusk is settling over the sound, I walk down to the dock to be by myself for a few minutes. I look across the sound and am saddened by what I see. Where once nothing but sand dunes broke the smoothness of the Outer Banks, big gray summer homes and condominiums now loom like distant battleships. Several water tanks even sprout like weeds beyond the eastern marshes where I once caught so many fish. Water tanks, for God's sake.

On the drive through Currituck County earlier this afternoon, my friends and I noticed that gift shops for tourists and twenty-four hour convenience stores have replaced many of the clapboard general stores that were here when we first started fishing Currituck Sound. Convenience stores and tourist gift shops, for God's sake. I turn my back on the sound, mope back into the hunting and fishing lodge, and mix a bourbon and water.

Early the next morning, Hugh Carpenter wakes us for our first day of fishing. It is raining; the gloom is appropriate for my mood. My friends and I don our rain jackets and dash across the yard to the dining room for breakfast. Curtis Youngblood asks the blessing. For a few seconds afterwards, nobody speaks. I wonder if the others are thinking, as am I, of our friends who once sat at this table with us but who are no longer living. Thankfully, Irene Carpenter interrupts my thoughts as she brings in hot dishes of food and places them on the lazy Susan at which we are seated.

This is something else that remains the same as it was in the old days, I realize, as we take turns spinning the table's carousel and snatching food from it: The food is still as delicious and as filling as the ones prepared by Evelyn Barrett (now Evelyn Barrett Meads) when she ran the lodge. We fishermen, as we always did, consume seconds and thirds of orange juice, eggs, grits, biscuits, sausage, bacon, homemade preserves, and pancakes and syrup. Irene and Hugh keep our cups filled with steaming coffee.

After breakfast, we return to our rooms to tend to our morning rituals. While we are doing this, our four guides arrive. Three young guides, none of whom I had ever met in the years that I fished the sound, are pulling big fiberglass runabouts, not traditional Currituck juniper-wood skiffs behind their trucks and automobiles. Fiberglass runabouts, for God's sake.

Last night, the eight fishermen in our party drew cards to see who would fish together and which guides we would have. I drew George Brumback, a newcomer to our group, as a partner and Johnny Owens as a guide. I tell George how lucky we are to have Johnny, one of the last of the old-time Currituck fishing guides. I know I will feel at home in his skiff. It is made of wood that has been lovingly and painstakingly cut, sawed, bent into shape, sanded, nailed, and glued—not poured from resin as are the fiberglass boats many of the youthful guides now use.

Johnny is a tall, straight-backed, middle-aged Air Force retiree whom sportswriter Wilt Browning once described as looking like the Marlboro Man. When Johnny sees George Brumback and me, his handsome sun-blackened, beard-stubbled face breaks into a wide grin. He sticks out his hand and pumps mine as hardily as if I were an old friend, which I feel I am. I introduce George, and we load our tackle in Johnny's ancient Ford. I climb in the crowded back and settle on, of all things, a new plastic toilet seat lid. Johnny explains that he just bought it and has not had time to put it on his commode yet. George gets in the front passenger seat, and Johnny drives to the Walnut Island Motel where he keeps his skiff in a weather-beaten shed at the terminus of a canal that leads to the sound.

If there are fish to be found, Johnny will know where they are, I tell George. I recall that Greensboro's Tom Fee and I were fishing with Johnny the day we both caught more fish than Roger Soles caught, one of the few times either Tom or I had ever done that. It was a memorable feat because Roger is one of the state's best bass fly rod anglers. Johnny was as proud as we were when he displayed our fish to the other guides that day.

But now as we load our tackle in the skiff, Johnny says, "I've guided only one fishing party all fall. And we didn't catch anything. Nobody is catching anything. I don't think there are many bass in the sound any more."

231

Johnny places two seat cushions on the middle seats and directs George and me to sit on them. He pumps the fuel line bulb of his outboard motor, unties the bow and stern lines and slips the skiff out of the shed, yanks the starter cord, and slowly steers out of the canal. Reaching open water, he races to a cluster of marshy islands where I once caught bass just about every time I fished it.

Arriving at the islands, Johnny shuts down the motor and directs us to take our casting positions. I tell George to take the first turn in the bow. Although he has never fished Currituck before, he has heard me brag about it over the years. For that reason, if there is to be only one fish caught on this day, I want him to catch it.

Johnny picks up his push pole and moves to the middle of the skiff. George and I fish hard for about thirty minutes without getting so much as a sniff from a fish. I ask Johnny what he thinks has happened to the bass in the sound. He says he is not sure but that he does not believe the salt is responsible for all the problem.

"I think it's pollution, all the shit they put into the sound," he adds. "Look at the water. It's even a different color from what it used to be."

He is right. The water is greenish-blue, not crystal clear as it was during most of the years I fished the sound.

Johnny interrupts my reveries when he uses his left hand to steady the boat with the shoving pole and points to the east with his right hand and says, "Look at those."

George and I hear the distant barking of Canada geese and see a long V etched against the sullen sky. It will take more than that to give Johnny hope.

"Hunting isn't even as good as it used to be,'" he says. "There aren't many ducks and geese anymore."

I drop my fly rod popping bug to a clump of grass protruding from the water off a marshy point. I jiggle my rod, telegraphing a signal down to the bug, which twitches as if it were alive. Then I pop the bug and continue to pop it for four or five feet before lifting it out of the water.

"I remember the time when, if you made a cast like that, you would expect to get a strike—and you often did," I tell George.

Johnny agrees.

"I believe you," George replies—as if he really does believe it.

The sky becomes more ominous, and a light drizzle begins to fall again. We scurry into our foul weather suits, and in a few minutes, heavy rain drums on the hoods of our jackets. It's about time for lunch anyway, so Johnny fires up his motor and speeds back to the shed. We sit in the shed and listen to the rain beating on the tin roof as we eat the ham sandwiches and cake and drink the coffee the Carpenters have prepared for us. The rain slacks a little.

"You want to try it again?' Johnny asks halfheartedly.

That says a lot about the sorry state of fishing on the sound now. Like all other good guides, Johnny is competitive and wants his anglers to catch fish. It's depressing when even he is no longer enthusiastic. We fish hard for several hours more and still do not get a strike.

It's almost a relief when another downpour comes; it gives me an excuse to suggest that we stop fishing for the day. Johnny obliges, and we are soon back at the hunting and fishing lodge. After George and I pay Johnny, he says: "I've been thinking. I believe I'll fish the North River tomorrow."

This, too, says a lot about the wretched state of fishing on the sound. In the past, the only time most Currituck guides resorted to fishing the North River was when a nor'easter blew water out of the sound and made fishing it impossible.

Now, there is reason to fish the North River even when there is plenty of water in Currituck. Although the river is only about ten miles from Currituck and is connected to the sound by the Intracoastal Waterway, it apparently has not been as severely affected by saltwater intrusion or pollution or whatever it is that has ruined Currituck Sound bass fishing. Fishing on the river is still generally good but nowhere near as good as Currituck fishing once was.

As much as I love Currituck, Johnny's decision to fish the North River makes me hope I draw him as a guide again the next day because I don't care to fish the sound again. Besides, I just enjoy fishing with Johnny, and I dread the thought of fishing from one of the fiberglass boats the other guides now use.

After drinks and dinner that night, the anglers in our party again draw cards for guides and fishing partners. I try to hide my glee when I again draw Johnny's name. My fishing partner will be the other newcomer to our group: Dave DuBuisson, editorial page editor of the Greensboro *News & Record*.

Sunlight streaming through my bedroom window the next morning wakes me while the others are still sleeping, and I put my bathrobe on over my pajamas and slip down to the edge of the sound. Although the sun is still behind the dunes across the sound, a pale luminescent pink streak advertises the coming of dawn. The day promises to be beautiful. Only a few innocent-looking clouds hang over the horizon. I slip back into my room. Soon Hugh Carpenter knocks on the door of our sleeping quarters.

"Breakfast will be ready in thirty minutes," he announces.

After breakfast, Johnny picks us up and drives to the canal behind the Riviera Motel, a canal that leads into the North River. His skiff is tied next to the dock behind the motel. A friend helped him haul the heavy boat the ten miles or so from Walnut Island to the canal the night before. After we load our gear, Johnny carefully guides the skiff out the narrow ditch to the open water of the river.

It is a picturesque river. In some places, it cuts through marshes. These stretches and the ponds off the river's main body remind me of Currituck Sound. In other places, the river is sheltered by moss-dripping cypress trees.

The Intracoastal Waterway runs down the North River, and we spend part of the day fishing in the wash of big yachts, all going south to Florida for the winter.

In contrast to yesterday, today turns out to be a perfect Indian summer day, the kind that makes fishing enjoyable even when you don't catch fish. To make the day even better, Dave DuBuisson and I catch a respectable number of fish: bream, largemouth bass, white perch, yellow perch, and chain pickerel.

That night after dinner, I walk by myself down to the dock and watch the strobe-like beams from the Currituck Lighthouse sweep the sky from across the sound and dance on the water. The heavens are cloudless and the legions of stars are so bright they look close enough for me to reach up and pluck some from the heavens.

I remember standing in this very same spot on another night like this. That was the night my father died after suffering a heart attack. Ed Barrett had come to rouse me out of my sleep to inform me. I walked out into the yard that night as three of my fishing buddies—Bill Black, Curtis Youngblood and Jimmie Jeffries—got up to drive me home. As we traveled the nearly three hundred miles from Currituck that night, I recalled the time I brought Dad to Currituck for a Father's Day present.

Dad and I had caught our limits before 1 P.M. Almost every time Dad caught one on his casting outfit, I would catch one a minute or so later on my fly rod. Dad had never seen me fish with a fly rod and, even though I was a grown man, he beamed every time I caught a fish. I had only learned to fly fish the year before.

In those days, Currituck was the ideal place for fly rod fishing. I can only remember a few days on the sound when I did not catch at least my limit of largemouth on a fly rod and a popper.

Now, years after Dad's death, as I stand alone in the darkness looking out again at the lights of the new condominiums on the east side of the sound, I am glad that my father was able to fish Currituck before it changed. But I am also sad that I will never be able to fish with him again.

I am sad for another reason. The fishing is so poor, I think as I watch the rays from the Currituck Lighthouse sweep across the sky, that I may never fish with Johnny Owens again.

Two years later I heard of Johnny Owen's death. Now, like the Currituck Sound I once knew and loved, Johnny and most of my other old fishing guides are part of the past.

Appendix A

Books for Fly Rod Anglers

Following is a list of representative books and videos that should be of interest to the fly fisherman. This is by no means a complete list, and others may be helpful, especially to the novice. Some of these may be out of print, but many should be stocked by the larger libraries in North Carolina.

The Angler's Book of Fly Tying and Fishing by Howard Goldberg

The Art and Science of Fly Fishing by Paul N. Fling

Basic Fly Fishing and Fly Tying by Ray Ovington

Book of Wet Fly Fishing by Vernon S. Hidy

Caddis Flies by Gary LaFontaine

Challenge of the Trout by Gary LaFontaine

The Complete Book of Fly Tying by Eric Leiser

The Dry Fly by Gary LaFontaine

Fishing the Fly as a Living Insect: An Unorthodox Method by Leonard M. Wright

Flies in the Water, Fish in the Air: A Personal Introduction by Jim Arnosky

Fly Fisherman's Primer by Charles Kunkel Fox

The Fly Fisher's Reader by Leonard M. Wright

Fly Fishing: A Beginner's Guide by David Lee

Fly Fishing Heresies; A New Gospel for American Anglers by Leonard M. Wright

Fly Fishing for Smallmouth Bass by Harry Murray

Fly Tying and Fly Fishing for Bass and Panfish by Tom Nixon

Fly Fishing Strategy by Doug Swisher and Carl Richards; illustrated by Dave Whitlock

Fly Fishing for Trout; A Guide for Adult Beginners by Richard W. Talleur

Fly Rodding for Bass by Joe Livingston

Fly Tackle: A Guide to the Tools of the Trade by Harmon Henkin

Inshore Fishing the Carolinas' Coasts by Bob Newman

Inshore Fly Fishing by Lou Tabory

In the Ring of the Rise by Vincent Marinaro

Introduction to Fly Fishing (L. L Bean video) with Dave Whitlock

The Masters of the Dry Fly by J. Michael Migel

Masters of the Nymph by J. Michael Migel, Leonard M. Wright, and Dave Whitlock

A Modern Dry-Fly Code by Vincent Marinaro

Modern Fly Fishing by Jim Casada

Nymphs: A Complete Guide to Naturals and Their Imitations by Ernest George Schwiebert

The Orvis Fly Fishing Guide by Tom Rosenbauer

The Practical Fly Fisherman by A.J. McClane

Rising Trout: a New Approach by Charles Kunkel Fox

Simplified Fly Fishing by S.R. Slaymaker

The Soft Hackle Fly by Sylvester Nemes

The Sports Afield Treasury of Fly Fishing by Tom Paugh

Streamer Fly Tying and Fishing by Joseph D. Bates, Jr.

Streamers and Bucktails, the Big Fish Flies by Joseph D. Bates

Top of the Water Techniques (video)

Trout by Ray Bergman

The Trout and the Fly: A New Approach by John Goddard and Clark Bryan

The Trout and the Fly by Ray Ovington

The Trout and the Stream by Charles E. Brooks

Trout Fishing the Southern Appalachians by J. Wayne Fears

Appendix B

Some Places to Order Tackle

Following is a list, in alphabetical order, of some companies from which the author or his friends have ordered fly fishing equipment and have had good results. Most, if not all, offer catalogs or price lists. Some, in addition to selling paraphernalia, offer books, fly fishing trips and fly fishing schools. Most have liberal return policies and deliver remarkably fast. Most, if not all, have toll-free (800) telephone numbers.

This is by no means a complete list, but is simply a list of those that the author or his friends can vouch for. Most people who deal in fly fishing equipment are, like most of their fly fishing customers, fine folks.

L. L. Bean, Inc., Freeport, ME 04033. An old-line and famous outdoor equipment and clothing mail order company. Offers its own line of rods, reels, lines and clothing in addition to some other brands.

Dan Bailey's, P. O. Box 1019, Livingston, MT. Another well-known dealer in quality flies, fly fishing and fly tying equipment, and components of rod building.

Bass Pro Shops, 1935 South Campbell, Springfield, MO 65898-0123. Does not specialize in fly fishing equipment, but does offers some excellent fly fishing supplies in addition to a wide range of other fishing equipment.

Cabela's, 812 13th Avenue, Sidney, NE 69160. Sells equipment in a variety of price ranges for many types of fishing, including fly fishing. Publishes one catalog especially for fly fishing.

Caylor Custom Flies, Route 2, Box 111, Todd, NC 28684. Fine flies at a reasonable price.

Clemmens, 444 Schantz Spring Road, Allentown, PA 18104. This company deals primarily in components for anglers, including fly rod anglers, who like to make their own equipment. The company also offers instruction books for do-it-yourselfers and some finished equipment for anglers, including fly rod anglers, and items for lure building and fly tying, to name just a few.

Gander Mountain, Inc., Box 248, Highway W, Wilmot, WI 53192. Another famous general outdoor mail order company that offers a limited amount of, but some very good and serviceable, fly fishing equipment at good prices.

Don Ray Howell, 712 Island Ford Road, Brevard, NC 28712. A wonderful fly fisherman and fly tyer and wonderful person from whom to order some fine flies. People from all over the country order flies from him.

Kaufmann's, P. O. Box 23032, Portland, OR 97281-3032. As with many of the other catalogs listed in this section, you can learn a lot just by browsing through this catalog. Kaufmann's also is a wonderful place from which to order flies, fly rods, fly reels and other paraphernalia.

Murray's Fly Shop, P. O. Box 156, Edinburg, VA 22824. Operated by fly fisherman Harry Murray, who is a well-known fly fisherman and writer about fly fishing. Catalog offers fly-fishing equipment by several top-of-the-line manufacturers and also some well-made, beautiful and deadly flies for several types of fishing.

Netcraft, 2800 Tremainsville Road, Toledo, OH 43613. Known more for other types of fishing equipment than for fly fishing equipment. Nevertheless, has some good fly fishing equipment, including some good bargains in do-it-yourself items. Author has made some very good casting fly rods from moderate-priced blanks and other items offered by the company.

Orvis, Historic Route 7A, Manchester, VT 05254. This is an old and well-known and well-respected concern which has the reputation of offering high-quality fishing equipment, outdoor clothing and other goods. Some individual dealers around the country offer some Orvis gear and Orvis has retail stores in various locations from which you can buy tackle or order it to get even faster service than if you order from the Manchester store. Orvis also apparently often fills orders sent to Orvis' Manchester headquarters from the nearest Orvis store to speed up delivery.

Westbank Anglers, P. O. Box 523, Teton Village, WY 83025. Located near fly fishing paradise of Jackson Hole, Wyoming. Good variety of flies and other top-of-the-line equipment for fly fishing.

Appendix C

An Essay on Catching Trout

Entire books have been written about fishing with dry flies. But this short essay tells about all you need to know to catch trout on top of the water. It was written by John Baskervill at the request of the Nat Greene Flyfishers club and was published in the club's newsletter. It is reprinted here with John's permission. John has the reputation of not mincing words and not wasting them either, a quality evident in this tract.

How to Catch Trout on Dry Flies in the Southern Appalachians

By John Baskervill

First, forget about ninety percent of what you read and hear from the out-of-town experts, who over-complicate a simple pastime in order to justify their own existence and reputation as experts.

Dress conservatively, wade quietly and stay in the shadows; skulk along in the bushes. If you throw your shadow or your rod's shadow on the water, you have already scared the fish before you make your first cast.

Learn to fish a short line, and make accurate casts with no line and very little leader on the water. It is impossible to control drag with a lot of line on the water. Always fish the cast out until the fly has floated all the way back to you.

Don't worry about matching the hatch. You won't see many hatches anyway. Use a fly you can see and one that floats well (Irresistible, Humpy, Wulff). I use a Number Twelve most of the time, occasionally a Number Eight or Number Ten—very seldom anything smaller than a Number Fourteen. Leaders around seven feet to nine feet 4x or 3x. These tippets get your fly back from streamside bushes much more efficiently than 6x or 8x tippets and will hold a good fish in close cover.

Learn where the trout live. They don't live out in the middle of the stream in the current. They live under things—rocks, logs, ledges, overhanging bushes, and they are not going to chase things very far from those places; hence, accuracy mentioned before. With a short line you can hold the fly stationary in dead spots and eddies, little places no larger than a dinner plate. If it stays in these places long enough, a fish will come up and get it.

Don't waste time. If you don't get a strike after two or three casts, you probably aren't going to. Go to the next spot. Plan how you are going to fish the next spot while you are fishing the one below it.

Utilizing these few simple ideas has caused the untimely demise of thousands of trout over a period of fifty-plus years.

Try them, and I believe you can increase your catch.

Appendix D

Finding Tar Heel Fly Fishing Spots

How do you find places to fish In North Carolina? Here are some sources, some of which may have toll-free (800) telephone numbers in addition to the number listed.

ADC Chartbook of North Carolina and other aids. The chartbook contains maps of eastern North Carolina waters showing depths, underwater obstructions, the types of fish that may be caught in different areas, boat ramps, marinas, airstrips, campgrounds and other facilities, roads and highways, and much other information. The same company that publishes the chartbook also publishes maps of some inland freshwater lakes and Eastern North Carolina brackish and saltwater areas. Maps show information that will help anglers. For information, including prices, call toll-free: 1-800-ADC-MAPS.

Blue Ridge Parkway, 700 BBT Building, One Pack Square, Asheville, NC 28801.

A Catalog of Inland Fishing Waters of North Carolina. This is a book that was based on a U.S. Government study, now old, of every creek, pond, lake, river, and sound that was in existence at the time the study was made. It reveals the results of a survey of anglers: the kind of fish they caught in many of the waters. It also shows boat access areas that were in existence at the time the study was made. While some of this information is now out of date, much of it is still helpful. The publication is out of print but some libraries still have it.

Cherokee Chamber of Commerce, Box 460, Cherokee, NC 28719. Contact this organization for information about fishing the thirty miles of trout streams on the Cherokee Indian Reservation.

Geodetic Survey Maps. U.S. Geodetic Survey, Reston, VA 22092. Maps show towns, roads, elevations, drainages, streams and other topographic features.

Great Smoky Mountains National Park, 115 Park Headquarters Road, Gatlinburg, TN 37738. Write this agency for information about fishing in both the North Carolina and Tennessee portions of the park.

National Forest Maps. National Forests in North Carolina, P. O. Box 2750, Asheville, NC 28802.

National Parks Fishing Guide by Robert Gartner. Stocked in some larger libraries.

North Carolina Atlas and Gazetteer. DeLorne Mapping, P. O. Box 298, Freeport, ME 04032. Includes maps and information about all public North Carolina waters from the mountains to the coast,including a page about trout waters.

North Carolina County Maps. C.J. Puetz, Puetz Place, Lyndon Station, WI 53944. Also shows roads and highways and gives other information.

N.C. Department of Commerce. Travel Development Division, 430 N. Salisbury St., Raleigh, NC 27604. From time to time, this state agency publishes information on fishing in North Carolina.

N.C. Division of Parks and Recreation, Public Information Office. P. O. Box 27687, Raleigh, NC 27611-7687. Good source of information about fishing in state parks.

The Roads of North Carolina. Sherear Publishing, 406 Post Oak Road, Fredericksburg, TX 78621. Shows all highways and roads and gives other information.

Wildlife Resources Commission, 512 N. Salisbury St., Raleigh, NC 27604. This agency enforces North Carolina game laws and regulations, issues hunting and fishing licenses, publishes information about game laws and regulations, and is the source of other types of information about hunting and fishing in the state. One of the finest sources of information about hunting and fishing and other outdoor recreation in the state is *Wildlife in North Carolina* magazine. You can subscribe to it by calling or writing the commission. Another good way to learn about fishing in the state is to go to a library that stocks back issues and read through them. The commission also publishes a list of boating access areas which may be obtained, as long as they are in stock, by writing the commission's Division of Boating and Inland Fisheries at the commission's address above.

Appendix E

Does the Moon Know About Fishing?

On fishing trips, a friend takes a lot of kidding about one subject.

"Hey," his fishing buddies ask, "when is the major period today?"

Or, when he and his friends are catching only a few fish, they ask, "Hey, is this a minor period?"

My friend suffers the joshing in good spirits. He knows the joke is often on the joker. On many days, my friend catches more fish than the people who kid him. And he almost always catches some fish.

He is, in fact, one of the best all-around anglers that I know. He is good with a fly rod. He is good with a spinning rod. He is good with a casting rod. He is good with natural bait. He is a good freshwater fisherman. He is a good saltwater fisherman.

Like most anglers, he will go fishing any time he can get away. But if he has a choice, he will schedule his trips so that he is on the water during "major periods." If he can't do that, he tries to arrange to arrive at his destinations in time for the "minor periods."

251

To him, and to other believers, a major period is the time during the day when the fish will usually—everything else being equal—hit the best. A minor period is the second best time for fishing.

So how does my friend know when major and minor periods will occur?

He carries the John Alden Knight Solunar Tables in his billfold, in a pocket of his fishing trousers, or in his fly fishing vest. The tables, based on such factors as the positions of the moon and sun, tell him the best times of the day—the major and minor periods—to fish. The tables, published in the sports pages of nearly two hundred major newspapers, list the best times of each day for fishing.

Knight got the idea for his Solunar Tables from something that happened to him on a 1926 bass fishing trip to Florida. He and his guide, Bob Wall, had not caught anything all morning. But Wall, looking at his watch, told Knight that the fish should start hitting in a short while. Wall said that was when the moon would be right.

Sure enough, the fish started hitting at the time Wall had predicted.

Knight, a real estate broker for a New York bank, was so intrigued that he eventually gave up his position with the bank to devote his full time to studying how the moon (and the sun) affects the habits of fish and to develop what would become known as the Solunar Tables.

("Solunar" is a combination of the words solar, meaning sun, and lunar, meaning moon.)

As most people know, the moon's pull causes ocean tides that affect the cycles during which saltwater fish feed. It made sense to Knight that the moon's pull could also affect the feeding habits of freshwater fish.

Officials at the New York Aquarium confirmed that their studies showed that this was a distinct possibility. Knight also consulted with scientists of several U.S. government agencies. Knight concluded that the sun (in conjunction with the moon) also had a bearing on the habits of freshwater fish.

After much study, he concluded that, on most days, two major periods and two minor periods occur. These periods last several hours each and the time of the day that they take place varies but can be predicted. They also happen at different times of the day in different areas of the country— just as ocean tides occur at different times in different areas. For that reason, Knight worked out a system so that the Solunar Tables could be adjusted for different parts of the country.

After John Alden Knight died, his son took over the compilation of the tables. After the son's death, the son's widow continued the work.

My friend who carries the Solunar Tables on fishing trips is not a superstitious person. He is an intelligent college graduate and is retired after a successful career in a financial field that required him to be coldly objective. Yet he is convinced from his own experience that the Solunar Tables are rooted in science.

And what angler doubts that there are times when fish bite and times when they don't?

On many days, you'll catch fish for several hours and then for several hours afterwards, you can't buy a strike.

And on many days you'll catch the bulk of your fish at the same times that anglers fishing other parts of the same river or lake catch most of their fish.

Of course, this doesn't happen every day. If conditions are poor for fishing you may not catch fish even during the "major" periods. On other rare days, you might catch fish all day long—not just during major and minor periods. But my friend believes that on most days, the Solunar Tables are a reliable guide to when you are most likely to catch fish.

Appendix F

Principal North Carolina Mountain Trout Waters

Wild Trout Waters

These are waters where, as of this writing, trout reproduce naturally. They have been were classified by the North Carolina Wildlife Resources Commission as "wild trout waters." Veteran anglers get a special thrill out of catching wild trout because, generally speaking, they fight harder. Some anglers can tell whether a trout is wild or from a hatchery just as soon as it hits.

Different regulations apply to different wild trout streams or even to different portions of some wild trout streams. For example, some streams or stretches of stream may be fished only with artificial lures, some with flies only, some with artificial lures with only one hook, and so on. Others may be fished with artificial lures or natural bait (excluding live fish). In some waters, all trout caught must be released. Some may be fished only at certain times of the day on certain dates. Also, regulations could change from year to year. All of these things are done so that the Wildlife Resources

Commission can manage trout fishing so as to make trout fishing a pastime that will last for generations to come. You should check up-to-date regulations before fishing any stream. Copies of regulations are available from agencies that sell state fishing licenses or from the Wildlife Resources Commission, 512 N. Salisbury St., Raleigh, NC 27604-1188.

Alleghany County:

Big Sandy Creek and Stone Mountain Creek (portions inside park)

Ramey Creek

Ashe County:

Big Horse Creek (Virginia line to State Road 1361 bridge, excluding tributaries)

Three Top Creek (Game Land portion)

Avery County:

Birchfield Creek

Cow Camp Creek

Cranberry Creek

Horse Creek

Jones Creek

Lost Cove Creek (Game Land portion, excluding Gragg Prong and Rockhouse Creek)

Kentucky Creek

North Harper Creek

Roaring Creek

Rockhouse Creek

South Harper Creek

Wilson Creek (Game Land portion)

Buncombe County:

Carter Creek (Game Land portion)

Burke County:

All streams in South Mountains State Park except the main part of Jacob Fork between the mouth of Shinny Creek and the lower park boundary

Caldwell County:

Buffalo Creek (headwaters to lower Dahl property line)

Joe Fork (Watauga County line to falls)

Rockhouse Creek

Cherokee County:

Tellico River (Fain Ford to Tennessee state line, excluding tributaries)

Clay County:

Buck Creek (Game Land portion downstream of U.S. Highway 64 bridge)

Graham County:

Deep Creek

Long Creek (Game Land portion)

Jackson County:

Chattooga River (State Road 1100 bridge to South Carolina line)

Flat Creek

Gage Creek

Lower Fowler Creek (Game Land portion)

Scotsman Creek (Game Land portion)

Tanasee Creek

Tuckasegee River (above Clark property)

Whitewater River (downstream from Silver Run Creek to South Carolina state line)

Wolf Creek (except Balsam Lake)

Macon County:

Chattooga River

Jarrett Creek (Game Land portion)

Kimsey Creek

Overflow Creek (Game Land portion)

Park Creek

Tellico Creek (Game Land portion)

Turtle Pond Creek (Game Land portion)

Mitchell County:

Green Creek (headwaters to Green Creek bridge)

Little Rock Creek (above Green Creek)

Wiles Creek (Game Land boundary to mouth)

McDowell County:

Newberry Creek (Game Land portion)

Transylvania County:

Davidson River (headwaters to Avery Creek, excluding Avery Creek, Grogan Creek, and Looking Glass Creek)

North Fork French Broad River (Game Land portions downstream of State Road 1392)

South Fork Mills River

Whitewater River (downstream from Silver Run Creek to South Carolina line)

Watauga County:

Boone Fork (portion between Blue Ridge Parkway boundary and Watauga River)

Dutch Creek (headwaters to second bridge on State Road 1134)

Howards Creek (headwaters to lower falls)

Watauga River (Avery County line to State Road 1559)

Wilkes County:

Big Sandy Creek, Garden Creek, and Widow Creek (portions in Stone Mountain Park)

Harris Creek (portion on Stone Mountain State Park)

Yancey County:

Lickskillet Creek

Middle Creek (Game Land boundary to mouth)

Rock Creek (Game Land boundary to mouth)

South Toe River (Game Land boundary downstream to Clear Creek)

South Toe River (portion from the concrete bridge above Black Mountain Campground downstream to Game Land boundary, excluding Camp Creek and Neals Creek)

Upper Creek and Lower Creek

Hatchery-Supported Waters

This list also changes from time to time as the Wildlife Resources Commission adds waters that it stocks. A few of these streams are classified as "delayed harvest" streams, which means that they are subject to special regulations. The commission lists the latest hatchery streams in its regulations digest that anglers can obtain at the time that they get their fishing licenses and trout stamps.

Alleghany County:

Big Glade Creek

Big Pine Creek

Bledsoe Creek

Brush Creek

Crab Creek

Cranberry Creek

Laurel Branch

Little Pine Creek

Little River (Whitehead to McCann dam)

Meadow Fork

Pine Swamp Creek

Piney Fork

Prather Creek

Water Falls Creek (South Fork Little River)

Ashe County:

Big Horse Creek (State Road 1361 to Tuckerdale)

Big Laurel Creek

Buffalo Creek (headwaters to junction of North Carolina 194–88 and State Road 1131)

Cranberry Creek (Alleghany County line to South Fork New River)

Helton Creek (Virginia line to New River)

Hoskins Fork (Watauga County line to North Fork New River)

Mill Creek

Nathans Creek

North Beaver Creek

North Fork New River (Watauga County line to Sharp dam)

Old Fields Creek

Peak Creek (headwaters to Trout Lake, except Blue Ridge Parkway waters)

Pine Swamp (all forks)

Roan Creek

South Beaver Creek (headwaters to Ashe Lake)

Three Top Creek (except Game Land portion)

Trout Lake

Avery County:

Archie Coffey Lake

Boyde Coffey Lake

Elk River (State Road 1306 crossing to the Tennessee state line)

Gragg Prong

Linville River (Land Harbor line below dam to Ben Aldridge line, except Bob Miller property)

Linville River (Sloop dam to Blue Ridge Parkway boundary line)

Mill Timber Creek

North Toe River (headwaters to Mitchell County line)

Plumtree Creek

Squirrel Creek

Webb Prong

Buncombe County:

Bent Creek (headwaters to N.C. Arboretum boundary line)

Big Ivy Creek [Ivy River] (Dillingham Creek to U.S. Highway 19–23 Bridge)

Cane Creek (headwaters to State Road 3138 bridge)

Corner Rock Creek

Dillingham Creek (Corner Rock Creek to Big Ivy Creek)

Lake Powhatan

Mineral Creek

Reems Creek (Sugar Camp Fork to U.S. Highway 19–23 bridge)

Stony Creek

Swannanoa River (State Road 2702 bridge near Ridgecrest to Sayles Bleachery in Asheville)

Burke County:

Carroll Creek (Game Lands above State Road 1405)

Henry Fork (lower Morganton watershed line downstream to State Road 1919 at Ivy Creek)

Jacobs Fork (Shinny Creek to lower South Mountains State Park boundary)

Linville River (Game Lands portion below the Blue Ridge Parkway and from first bridge on State Road 1223 below Lake James powerhouse to Muddy Creek)

Caldwell County:

Boone Fork Pond

Thorpe Creek (falls to N.C. Highway 90 bridge)

Wilson Creek (Phillips Branch to Brown Mountain Beach dam)

Cherokee County:

Bald Creek

Beaver Dam Creek (headwaters to State Road 1326 bridge)

Davis Creek

Hyatt Creek

Junaluska Creek (Ashturn Creek to Valley River)

North Shoal Creek [Cane Creek] (headwaters to State Road 1325)

Persimmon Creek

Shuler Creek

Valley River

Webb Creek

Clay County:

Fires Creek (fish barrier to State Road 1300)

Hothouse Branch

Shooting Creek (headwaters to U.S. Highway 64 bridge at State Road 1338)

Tuni Creek

Tusquitee Creek (headwaters to lower State Road 1300 bridge)

Vineyard Creek

Graham County:

Big Snowbird Creek (old railroad junction to mouth)

Calderwood Reservoir (Cheoah dam to Tennessee line)

Cheoah Reservoir

Franks Creek

Huffman Creek (Little Buffalo Creek)

Long Creek (portion not on Game Lands)

Mountain Creek (Game Lands boundary to State Road 1138 bridge)

Panther Creek

Santeetlah Creek (Johns Branch to mouth)

Sawyer Creek

South Fork Squalla Creek

Squalla Creek

Stecoah Creek

Talula Creek (headwaters to lower bridge on State Road 1211)

West Buffalo Creek

Yellow Creek

Haywood County:

Cold Springs Creek

Hemphill Creek

Hurricane Creek

Jonathans Creek, lower (concrete bridge in Dellwood to Pigeon River)

Jonathans Creek, upper (State Road 1302 bridge [west] to State Road 1307 bridge)

Richland Creek (Russ Avenue bridge to U.S. Highway 19A–23 bridge)

West Fork Pigeon River (headwaters to Champion International property line, except Middle Prong)

Henderson County:

Big Hungry River

Camp Creek (State Road 1919 to Polk County line)

Green River, upper (mouth of Bob Creek to mouth of Rock Creek and Lake Summit dam to Polk County line)

Little Hungry River

North Fork Mills River (Game Land portion below the Hendersonville watershed dam)

Rocky Broad River (half mile north of Bat Cave to Rutherford County line)

Jackson County:

Balsam Lake

Bear Creek Lake

Buff Creek (State Road 1457 bridge below Bill Johnson's property to Scott Creek)

Cullowhee Creek (Tilley Creek to Tuckasegee River)

Dark Ridge Creek (Jones Creek to Scotts Creek)

Green's Creek (Green's Creek Baptist Church on State Road 1730 to Savannah Creek)

North Fork, Scott Creek

Savannah Creek (headwaters to Bradley's Packing House on N.C. Highway 116)

Scott Creek

Tanasee Creek Lake

Tuckasegee River (from confluence with West Fork Tuck-asegee River to N.C. Highway 107 bridge at Love Field and from N.C. Highway 116 bridge at Webster to State Road 1392 bridge at Wilmot)

Tuckasegee River (N.C. Highway 107 bridge at Love Field to N.C. Highway 116 bridge at Webster)

West Fork, Tuckasegee River (Shoal Creek to water level of Little Glenville Lake)

Wolf Creek Lake

Macon County:

Big Creek (base of Falls to Georgia state line)

Burningtown Creek

Cartoogechaye Creek (U.S. Highway 64 bridge to Little Tennessee River)

Cliffside Lake

Cullasaja River (Sequoah dam to U.S. Highway 64 bridge near junction of State Road 1672)

Ellijay Creek

Nantahala River (Nantahala dam to Whiteoak Creek)

Nantahala River (Whiteoak Creek to NP&L powerhouse discharge canal)

Queens Creek Lake

Roaring Fork Creek (Game Land boundary to mouth)

Tessentee Creek (Nichols Branch to Little Tennessee River)

Madison County:

Big Creek (headwaters to lower game land boundary)

Big Laurel Creek (Mars Hill watershed boundary to Rice's Mill Dam)

Little Creek

Max Patch Pond

Meadow Ford Creek (except Little Creek)

Mill Creek

Mill Ridge Pond

Puncheon Fork (Hampton Creek to Big Laurel Creek)

Roaring Fork

Shelton Laurel Creek (headwaters to N.C. Highway 208 Bridge)

Shut-in Creek

Spillcorn Creek

Spring Creek (junction of N.C. Highways 209 and 63 to lower U.S. Forest Service boundary line)

McDowell County:

Armstrong Creek (Cato Holler lower line downstream to Greenlee upper line)

Curtis Creek (fish barrier to U.S. Highway 70 bridge)

Little Buck Creek (Game Land portion)

Mill Creek (upper railroad bridge to U.S. Highway 70 bridge)

North Fork Catawba River (headwaters to North Cove School, State Road 1569)

Mitchell County:

Big Rock Creek (headwaters to fishing club property above A. D. Harrel farm)

Cane Creek (State Road 1219 to Nolichucky River)

East Fork Grassy Creek

Grassy Creek (East Fork Grassy Creek to mouth)

Little Rock Creek (Green Creek bridge to Big Rock Creek)

North Toe River (Avery County line to State Road 1121, also known as Altapass Road)

Polk County:

Big Fall Creek (portion above and below water supply reservoir)

Camp Creek (Henderson County line to Green River)

Cove Creek

Fork Creek (Fork Creek Church on State Road 1128 to North Pacolet River)

Fulloms Creek (State Road 1154 to Green River)

Green River (Henderson County line to mouth of Brights Creek)

Little Cove Creek

North Pacolet River (Pacolet Falls to N.C. Highway 108 bridge)

Rutherford County:

Rocky Broad River (Henderson County line to head of rapids at Goose Pond Hole)

Stokes County:

Dan River (lower Flippin property line below State Road 1416 to 200 yards downstream from end of State Road 1421)

Surry County:

Ararat River (State Road 1727 downstream to Business U.S. Highway 52 bridge)

Fisher River [Cooper Creek] (Virginia line to N.C. Highway 89 bridge)

Little Fisher River (Virginia state line to N.C. Highway 89 bridge)

Pauls Creek (Virginia line to State Road 1625)

Swain County:

Alarka Creek

Calderwood Reservoir (Cheoah dam to Tennessee line)

Cheoah Reservoir

Connelly Creek

Deep Creek (Great Smoky Mountains National Park boundary line to Tuckasegee River)

Nantahala River (Macon County line to Fontana Lake water level)

Transylvania County:

Davidson River (Avery Creek to Ecusta intake)

East Fork French Broad River (Glady Branch to French Broad River)

French Broad River (junction of west and north forks to U.S. Highway 276 bridge)

Middle Fork French Broad River

Thompson River (State Road 1152 to South Carolina state line)

West Fork French Broad River (State Road 1312 and State Road 1309 intersection to junction of west and north forks)

Watauga County:

Beech Creek

Boone Fork (headwaters to State Road 1562)

Buckeye Creek Reservoir

Coffee Lake

Cove Creek (State Road 1233 bridge at Zionville to State Road 1233 bridge at Amantha)

Dutch Creek (second bridge on State Road 1134)

Elk Creek (headwaters to gravel pit on State Road 1508)

Howards Creek (downstream from lower falls)

Laurel Creek

Maine Branch (headwaters to North Fork New River)

Meat Camp Creek

Middle Fork New River (Lake Chetola dam to South Fork New River)

Norris Fork Creek

North Fork New River (from confluence with Maine and Mine branches to Ashe County line)

Stony Fork (headwaters to Wilkes County line)

Watauga River (State Road 1559 bridge at Foscoe downstream to N.C. Highway 105 bridge)

Wilkes County:

Boundary Line Pond

East Prong Roaring River (lower state park boundary to Brewers Mill on State Road 1943)

East Prong Roaring River (mouth of Bullhead Creek downstream to Stone Mountain State Park boundary line)

Fall Creek

Harris Creek (end of State Road 1736 to mouth)

Middle Fork Reddies River [Clear Prong] (headwaters to bridge on State Road 1580)

Middle Prong Roaring River (headwaters to second bridge on State Road 1736)

North Fork Reddies River [Vannoy Creek] (headwaters to Union School bridge on State Road 1559)

North Prong Reddies River [Darnell Creek] (downstream ford on State Road 1569 to confluence with North Fork)

Pell Branch Pond

Pike Creek

Pike Creek Pond

South Fork Reddies River (headwaters to N.C. Highway 16 bridge)

South Prong Lewis Fork (headwaters to Lewis Fork Baptist Church)

Stone Mountain Creek (from falls at Alleghany County line to confluence with East Prong Roaring River and Bullhead Creek)

Stony Fork Creek (headwaters to Mt. Zion bridge near intersection of State Road 1155 and State Road 1167)

Yancey County:

Bald Mountain Creek

Cane River (Cattail Creek to Bowlens Creek)

Price Creek (junction of State Road 1120 and State Road 1121 to Indian Creek)

South Toe River (Clear Creek to lower boundary line of Yancey County recreation park)

State Game Lands

There are many good trout streams on North Carolina Game Lands in the mountains. Game Lands are tracts that are managed by the N.C. Wildlife Resources Commission. Most of Game Land trout streams hold wild trout. For information on fishing these streams, check the latest regulations digest that is available at state hunting and fishing license agencies or contact the N.C. Wildlife Resources Commission.

Note: N.C. State Parks, two of which contain fine trout fishing, are separate from Game Lands. Information on this fishing may be obtained by calling South Mountains State Park: (704) 433-4772 or Stone Mountain State Park: (919) 957-8185.

Other Trout Fishing

Great Smoky Mountains National Park—Some fine trout fishing is to be found on National Park Service land in the North Carolina mountains. For information on this fishing, contact:

Great Smoky Mountains National Park

107 Park Headquarters Road

Gatlinburg, TN 37738

(615) 436-1200

Cherokee Indian Reservation—Fishing on Cherokee Indian Reservation land is subject to permit from the Cherokee tribe. Many of the waters are heavily stocked. For information this fishing, contact:

Cherokee Fish and Game Management.

P. O. Box 302

Cherokee, NC 28719

(704) 497-5201

Blue Ridge Parkway Trout—For information on fishing Blue Ridge Parkway streams, contact:

Resource Management Specialist
Blue Ridge Parkway
200 BB&T Building
Asheville, NC 28801
(704) 271-4760

Index

Roaring River, 86

robin redbreast, 35–49

Rochelle, Jack, 19

Rockingham County, N.C., 58

Rocky Mount, N.C., 198

Royal Wulff fly, 105, 246

Rucker, John, 133–135

Rutherford County, N.C., 124

Rutherfordton, N.C., 103

S

Salazar, Amy, 220

Salazar, Paul, 109, 218–222

Salisbury, N.C., 41

salmon fly (*see* Bomber)

saltwater fish (*see* Eastern North Carolina)

Sanders, Newland, 105

Santee–Cooper lakes, 148

Santeetlah Lake, 42

Santeetlah River, 124

Satterfield, Ed, 4

Sawyer, Grover Cleveland "G.C.", Jr., 15

Scranton Creek, 76, 173–177

sea trout, 9, 129–135, 186–187, 188–191

shad, anadromous, 197–199

Sheep Fly 104–105, 154

"short–lining," 111–117

Smith, Bill, 50

Smith Mountain Lake (Virginia), 89

Smoky Mountains, 124, 248, 277

Snake Mountain, 18

Snead, Sam, 183

Snook, 197

Soles, Roger, 3, 13–16, 22, 42, 45, 50, 52, 54, 72, 231

Soles, Majelle, 16

Solunar Tables, 251–254

South Creek, 135

South River, 135

South Toe River, 86, 103, 124

Sox, the Reverend Sam, 214–218

spinner fly, 57, 58, 81, 95, 181, 199

split shot (for weight), 73, 131

Spruce Pine, N.C., 103

Spruill, Booty, 172

Staley, N.C., 89

Stanbery, Larry, 82–83

Statesville, N.C., 41

Staunton River (Virginia) 148

Stella, N.C., 61

Stephenson, Duncan, 229

Stokes County, N.C., 124

Stone Fly (*see* "Don's Stone Fly")

streamer fly 55, 74, 76, 77, 109, 131, 165, 168, 173–200, 207–208

strike indicator

Suggs, Bob, 35–37

Sumner, Emmett, 185

sunfish, green, 49

sunfish (*see* panfish)

sunfish, longear, 49

Superfly, 104

Surry County, N.C., 124

Swain County, N.C., 124

Swansboro, N.C., 61

Y

Yadkin River impoundments, 164,
    168, 170, 181, 207
Yancey County, N.C., 124
Yates, Bill, 68–70
Yellow Hammer nymph fly, 104
Yellow Stone fly, 104
Youngblood, Curtis, 20, 52, 61,
    158, 185, 235

Z

Zara Spook lure, 150
Zonker streamer, 92, 95, 160, 161,
    163, 170, 178, 180